Drawing

CW00363199

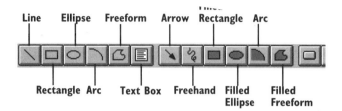

Line Ellipse Freeform Arrow Rectangle Arc

Rectangle Arc Text Box Freehand Filled Ellipse Filled Freeform

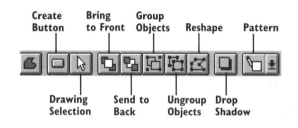

Create Button Bring to Front Group Objects Reshape Pattern

Drawing Selection Send to Back Ungroup Objects Drop Shadow

Chart toolbar

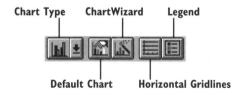

Chart Type ChartWizard Legend

Default Chart Horizontal Gridlines

Excel for Windows
Quick & Easy Reference

Excel for Windows™
Quick & Easy Reference

Douglas Hergert

San Francisco
Paris
Düsseldorf
Soest

SYBEX®

Developmental Editor: Richard Mills
Editor: Guy Hart-Davis
Technical Editor: Ellen Lawson Ferlazzo
Typesetter: Guy Hart-Davis
Proofreader/Production Coordinator: Janet K. Boone
Indexer: Paul Kish
Cover Designer: Archer Design
Cover Illustrator: Richard Miller

Screen reproductions produced with Collage Plus.
Collage Plus is a trademark of Inner Media Inc.

SYBEX is a registered trademark of SYBEX Inc.

TRADEMARKS: SYBEX has attempted throughout this book to distinguish
proprietary trademarks from descriptive terms by following the
capitalization style used by the manufacturer.

SYBEX is not affiliated with any manufacturer.

Every effort has been made to supply complete and accurate information.
However, SYBEX assumes no responsibility for its use, nor for any
infringement of the intellectual property rights of third parties which
would result from such use.

Library of Congress Card Number: 93-87418
ISBN: 0-7821-1378-8
Manufactured in the United States of America
10 9 8 7 6 5 4 3 2 1

ACKNOWLEDGMENTS

My sincere thanks to Guy Hart-Davis, Richard Mills, Joanne Cuthbertson, and Rudolph Langer for their ideas and suggestions; and to Erik Ingenito, Ellen Ferlazzo, Janet Boone, and Paul Kish for their contributions. Thanks also to Claudette Moore of Moore Literary Agency.

TABLE OF CONTENTS

INTRODUCTION

Microsoft Excel is the popular Windows spreadsheet program that provides worksheets, charts, databases, and list operations all in one software environment. In version 5, Excel takes many important steps forward in the simplicity of its procedures. Microsoft has added a variety of tools designed to make your work more efficient—streamlined workbook documents, special worksheet operations, ease-of-use enhancements, and new online help features.

Excel for Windows Quick & Easy Reference gives you succinct, accessible instructions for everyday tasks you'll want to accomplish in Excel. You'll find the information you need to complete your work with accuracy and understanding. Entries provide step-by-step procedures, shortcuts, examples, notes on usage, and cross references to related tasks. The goal is to help you work more efficiently and effectively with workbooks, worksheets, charts, lists, and databases.

New Features in Excel 5

As you begin working in Excel 5, the first major change you'll notice is the use of workbooks as the basic document type. A workbook is a convenient storage unit for the worksheets and charts you develop in Excel. In one workbook you create any number of interrelated sheets. (For more information, turn to the *Workbooks* entry on page 120.)

Because a workbook contains multiple sheets, you'll want to learn how to share and update data from one worksheet to another. Excel 5 allows you to create formulas that extend across worksheets in a book—including 3-D formulas, which you can use to summarize periodic data stored in several adjacent worksheets. In addition, the names you create in the sheets of a workbook have book-level scope by default. This means that one worksheet can refer by name to data located on other sheets. The convenient new Name box on the Formula bar gives you a list of all the book-level names in a workbook. (For more information, see *Formulas* [page 57], *Links and 3-D References* [page 67], *Names* [page 76], and *Workbooks* [page 120].)

Database features in spreadsheet programs sometimes seem like afterthoughts—but this is far from the case with Excel 5. You now define a list or a database simply by entering a row of field names followed by rows of records. Once you've created a database on a worksheet, sophisticated data operations are just a mouse click or a menu selection away. As in Excel 4, you can view, edit, and append individual records by opening a data form. With the AutoFilter feature you examine groups of records that match conditions that you select. You can instantly sort your database simply by selecting a key field and clicking one of the two Sort buttons. (See *Data Form* [page 30], *Database* [page 36], *Filters* [page 46], *Lists* [page 72], and *Sorting* [page 112] for more information.)

Charting has always been one of Excel's strengths, and this new release gives you even greater charting capabilities. The ChartWizard provides the most convenient techniques for developing chart sheets or embedded charts from a selection of worksheet data. Many options are available for making a chart look exactly the way you want it. (See *Charting* [page 10] and *ChartWizard* [page 16] for instructions and information.)

Alignment

Using the **Alignment** options in the **Format Cells** dialog box, you can change the alignment and orientation of text and numeric entries in a cell or a range of cells. For example, entries can be left- or right-justified, or centered.

To Change the Alignment of Entries in a Cell or Range

1. Select the cell or range of cells that you want to realign.

2. Choose **Format** ➤ **Cells**. In the **Format Cells** dialog box, click the **Alignment** tab. The **Alignment** dialog box appears on the screen.

3. In the **Horizontal** box, select the **Left**, **Center**, or **Right** option to change the alignment of text and numeric entries within the current column width settings.

4. Optionally, choose **Top**, **Center**, or **Bottom** in the **Vertical** box to adjust the placement of entries within the current row height.

5. Click **OK**.

 shortcut

To realign entries horizontally, you can select a cell or a range of cells and then click one of the three alignment buttons in the Formatting Toolbar—**Align Left**, **Center Align**, or **Align Right**. Alternatively, point to a cell or range and click the right mouse button to display the shortcut menu for the selection.

Choose **Format Cells**; then click the **Alignment** tab in the
Format Cells dialog box.

 **techno note**

The **General** option in the **Horizontal** box represents the default alignment settings: left-alignment for text entries, right-
alignment for numeric entries, and centering for logical and
error values.

 reminder

You can change the width or a column or the height of a row
by dragging a line in the corresponding column heading or
row heading. (See *Column Width* on page 23 and *Row Height* on
page 103 for details.) When you do so, Excel adjusts the alignment of entries according to the current selections in the
Alignment dialog box. For example, if you increase the column width for a range of centered entries, Excel centers the
entries within the new width.

To Rotate Entries within Cells

1. Select the cell or range of cells that you want to rotate.

2. Choose **Format** ➢ **Cells**, and click the **Alignment** tab.

3. Select one of the samples displayed in the **Orientation**
box—for text arranged vertically, text rotated to read from
bottom to top, or text rotated to read from top to bottom.

4. Click **OK**.

tip

Excel automatically adjusts the row height to accommodate the length of a rotated entry. If you later restore the default horizontal orientation, you may also want to restore the appropriate row height by double-clicking the line below the corresponding row heading.

To Justify a Long Text Entry within its Cell

1. Select the cell containing the long text entry that you want to justify.

2. Choose **Format** ➢ **Cells** and click the **Alignment** tab.

3. Select the **Justify** option in the **Horizontal** box. Then click **OK**. In response, Excel wraps the text within the cell, increasing the row height as necessary. To the extent possible, the text is aligned along the left and right sides of the cell.

4. Optionally, adjust the column width and row height at the cell's location to achieve the justified text arrangement that you want.

Arithmetic Operations

To build arithmetic formulas in Excel, you can use any combination of the four familiar operations—addition, subtraction, multiplication, and division. Excel also supports exponentiation and percentage operations.

AUTOFILL

To Write an Arithmetic Formula

Use any combination of the following operands:

+   addition

-     subtraction

*   multiplication

/   division

%   percentage

^   exponentiation

 **techno note**

In a formula that contains more than one arithmetic operand, Excel performs operations in this order: percentage, exponentiation, multiplication and division (left to right), addition and subtraction (left to right). Use parentheses in a formula to override this default order of operations. For example, in the following formula, the names INCOME, EXPENSES, and TAXRATE represent three different cells on the current worksheet:

    =(INCOME-EXPENSES)*TAXRATE%

To evaluate this formula, Excel performs the percentage operation first (dividing the value of TAXRATE by 100), then the subtraction (enclosed in parentheses), and finally the multiplication.

AutoFill

By dragging the fill handle—the small black box at the lower-right corner of a selected cell or range—you can easily create series, copy data, or replicate formulas across rows or down

4

columns in the worksheet. In this context, a series is a sequence of numbers or dates in which the difference between any one entry and the next is constant.

To Create a Series
by Dragging the Fill Handle

1. In consecutive cells of a column or adjacent cells of a row, enter the initial numeric or date elements of the series that you want to create. For example, enter **1** and **2** or **7/5/94** and **7/12/94** in a pair of neighboring cells.

2. Select the range of cells containing these entries.

3. Position the mouse pointer over the fill handle for the current selection. The pointer changes to a cross-hair shape.

4. Drag the mouse down or across to the cells where you want to extend the series. Excel fills the selection with the series you defined in the initial cell entries.

 tip

To fill a column or row with an identical sequence of entries—rather than a series—hold down Ctrl while you drag the fill handle. For example, imagine that you want to fill the range A1:A12 with repetitions of the labels **Product 1**, **Product 2**, and **Product 3**. To do so, enter these three labels into A1, A2, and A3. Then select A1:A3 and hold down Ctrl while you drag the fill handle from A3 to A12.

reminder

You can also drag the fill handle to copy a formula from an initial cell to consecutive cells down a column or adjacent cells across a row. If the formula contains relative references, Excel adjusts the references accordingly as it copies the formula to new positions. See *Copying Formulas* on page 28 for details.

AutoFormat

In the **AutoFormat** command, Excel provides you with over a dozen attractive formats that you can choose from for displaying and printing data in a worksheet. These designs include specific selections from Excel's formatting options—including borders, fonts, patterns, alignments, and numeric formatting, as well as adjustments in column widths and row heights. If one of the available designs suits the data you have entered into a given worksheet, you can save a lot of time by selecting the format directly from the AutoFormat dialog box rather than applying format options individually.

To Use the AutoFormat Feature

1. Select the table of data where you want to apply a pre-designed format. (Or select a single cell within the data table, and Excel will select the contiguous table range.)

2. Choose **Format ➤ AutoFormat**. The **AutoFormat** dialog box appears on the screen.

3. Select the name of a predesigned table format in the **Table Format** list, and examine the sample of the selected format that appears in the **Sample** box.

4. Repeat step 3 until you find a format that suits the current data table. Then click **OK** to apply this format to your data.

 tip

If you wish to apply only certain parts of a predesigned format to your data table, click the **Options** button on the **AutoFormat** dialog box. In response, the dialog box expands to display six check boxes labeled **Number**, **Border**, **Font**, **Pattern**, **Alignment**, and **Width/Height**. By default, all of these options are checked. Click a check box to remove the X and disable a given category of formatting.

Borders

Using the **Border** option in the **Format Cells** dialog box, you can draw a border around the perimeter of a selected range of cells in a worksheet, or around the individual cells within a selection. Alternatively, you can draw borders along specified sides of cells in a range. You can select from a variety of border styles and colors.

To Draw Borders

1. Select the range of cells where you want to create a border.

2. Choose **Format ➤ Cells**. Click the **Border** tab. The resulting dialog box contains a list of border locations and a group of available border styles.

3. From the **Border** options, select the location for a border you want to draw: The **Outline** option draws a border around the perimeter of the current range selection.

The **Left**, **Right**, **Top**, and **Bottom** options apply borders to all the cells within the current range.

4. From the **Style** options, select a border style for the current Border location. Eight style options are available: dotted, thin, medium, thick, double, small dashed, long dashed, and none.

5. Optionally, select **Color** list and select a color for the current border style.

6. Repeat steps 3 to 5 for each additional location where you want to apply a border. Note that you can apply different border styles and colors to particular locations within the current range of cells.

7. Click **OK** to apply the borders you have selected.

 shortcut

To view the **Border** options, click the right mouse button over a selected range of cells; then choose **Format Cells** from the resulting shortcut menu and click on the **Border** tab. Alternatively, select a range of cells and click the down-arrow next to the **Borders** button on the Formatting toolbar. Make a selection from the palette of border options that appears beneath the button. (This is a *tear-off palette*—you can drag it away from the button and keep it on the screen if you want to apply borders to several ranges on a worksheet.)

To Remove a Border

1. Select the range of cells that contain the border you want to remove.

2. Choose **Format** ➢ **Cells** and click the **Border** tab.

3. In the **Style** frame, select the no-border option. Then, in the **Border** frame, select each of the locations where you want to remove the border.

4. Click **OK**.

shortcut

Select the range of cells where you want to remove the borders, and press **Ctrl-Shift-hyphen** to remove all borders from the range, or click the down-arrow next to the Border button and select the no-border option from the **Border** palette.

Centering across Columns

You can center a title (or any other entry in a worksheet) across a horizontal range of cells.

To Center an Entry across a Range of Columns

1. Starting from the cell that contains a text or numeric entry, select a horizontal range of cells. The selected cells to the right of the entry should be blank.

2. Select **Format** ➢ **Cells** and click the **Alignment** tab. In the list of **Horizontal** options, choose **Center across selection**. Then click **OK**. Excel centers the entry across the range you have selected.

shortcut

Select a range of cells and click the **Center Across Columns** button on the Formatting toolbar.

warning

For editing and formatting purposes, a centered entry belongs to the cell where you originally entered it. This can become a little confusing when the entry *appears* to be located in a cell to the right of where the entry is actually stored.

Charting

⊛ ⊛ ⊛ ⊛ ⊛ ⊛ ⊛ ⊛ ⊛ ⊛ ⊛ ⊛ ⊛ ⊛ ⊛ ⊛ ⊛ ⊛ ⊛

An Excel chart is based on a table of numeric data and labels in a worksheet. A chart can be embedded in a worksheet, or it can appear in a separate window of its own. Either way, Excel gives you a great variety of chart types and formats to choose from. The first step in creating a chart is to select a range of worksheet data. Then you can use any of several simple techniques for creating the chart.

reminder

See *ChartWizard* on page 16 for an alternate approach to creating charts.

To Create an Embedded Chart

1. If the Chart toolbar is not currently displayed, point to any toolbar, click the right mouse button, and choose **Chart** from the resulting shortcut menu.

2. Select the worksheet data from which you want to create the chart. If you want Excel to copy labels to the chart from your worksheet, include a row and/or column of text entries in your range selection.

3. Click the arrow next to the **Chart Type** button in the **Chart** toolbar and select the chart type you want. Then move the mouse pointer back to the worksheet; the pointer appears in a crosshair shape with a small chart icon.

4. Drag the mouse pointer over the worksheet area where you want to display the chart. Release the mouse button when you have defined an appropriate area for the chart. Excel draws the embedded chart on your worksheet.

5. If you are not satisfied with the chart as it initially appears, experiment with other chart types by selecting them from the **Chart Type** list as in step 3.

Figure 1 shows an example of an embedded chart, based on the data displayed in the range A1:F3. Each pair of columns in the chart represents the admission offers and enrollment of a school. Notice that Excel automatically displays labels from row 1 along the chart's horizontal axis, known as the *x-axis*. The legend (at the right side of the chart) displays labels from column A of the worksheet.

 tip

While you drag the mouse over the worksheet area where you want to display the chart, you can hold down **Shift** to create a square chart box. Alternatively, hold down **Alt** to create a chart box aligned with the worksheet grid.

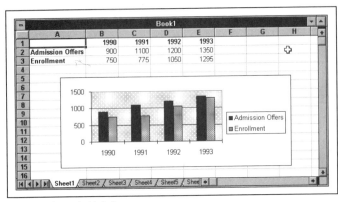

FIGURE 1: *An embedded chart*

 techno note

You typically create a chart from a single contiguous range of worksheet cells, but Excel can also create a chart from nonadjacent ranges—as long as the range dimensions together form a usable data table. See *Selecting a Range* on page 106 to learn how to select nonadjacent cells.

 **tip**

Select an embedded chart by clicking it with the mouse. When an embedded chart is selected, Excel displays *selection handles*—small black squares—around the perimeter of the chart box. (Excel also normally displays the Chart toolbar when an embedded chart is selected.) You can change the size of the embedded chart by dragging any one of its selection handles, or you can move the chart to a new position in the worksheet by dragging the entire chart box with the mouse. Delete an embedded chart by selecting it and pressing the **Del** key. Deselect an embedded chart by clicking elsewhere in the worksheet.

12

To Edit and Format an Embedded Chart

1. Double-click the embedded chart. In response, Excel displays a thick border around the chart. (If the chart is too large to appear on the screen, Excel instead copies the chart to a temporary window; the name of this window consists of the name of the source worksheet itself followed by a generic chart name such as Chart 1, Chart 2, and so on.)

2. When a chart is active, a number of chart-related commands are available in the Excel menus. Choose commands from the **Insert** and **Format** menus to make changes in the appearance of the chart.

- The **Insert** menu allows you to add new items to your chart, including titles, labels, a legend, and gridlines.

- The **Format** menu contains commands for changing the appearance of the entire chart (**Chart Type** and **AutoFormat**) or of selected items in the chart.

 shortcut

To change the chart type, you can simply select the chart and click the arrow next to the **Chart Type** button on the Chart toolbar. Then select a new chart type from the palette shown. Alternatively, to choose from a larger selection of chart types, double-click the embedded chart and then choose **Format ➤ AutoFormat**. The resulting dialog box offers over a dozen *galleries* of chart types. For example, Figure 2 displays the enrollment chart (originally shown in Figure 1) in a new format. The admission offers are still represented as columns in the chart, but the enrollment is now represented as a line. This is known as a *combination* chart.

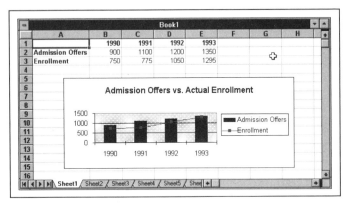

FIGURE 2: *Changing the chart type*

 tip

You can select individual items or areas of an active chart for editing. To do so, click the item or area with the mouse; Excel displays selection handles around or within the element that you select. For example, you can select the entire chart area, the plot area, an axis, the legend, or the chart title. After selecting an item in the chart, pull down the **Format** menu and choose the **Selected** command to see the list of the relevant formatting options.

Alternatively, point to a chart item and press the right mouse button to view a shortcut menu of commands that apply to the selection. Or double-click any chart item to view the **Format** dialog box for that item.

 **techno note**

You can also select a *series* in the chart—that is, all the chart markers representing a particular range of numbers from the source worksheet table. When you do so, the formula bar shows the *series formula* that links the series to the corresponding worksheet range. The series formula consists of a call to Excel's built in SERIES function, which defines the link between the chart and the source worksheet data.

 reminder

You can use the ChartWizard as a guide for all the steps of creating a chart; see *ChartWizard* on page 16 for details.

 reminder

When a chart object is active you can print the chart by choosing **File ➢ Print** or by clicking the **Print** tool in the Standard toolbar. (See *Printing Charts* on page 91 for more information.)

To Create a New Chart Sheet

1. In the source worksheet, select the range of data from which you want to create a new chart.

2. Choose **Insert ➢ Chart**. In the **Chart** submenu, choose **As New Sheet**.

3. The first **ChartWizard** dialog box appears on the

screen. Click **Finish** to produce a chart in the default format, or work through all five ChartWizard steps as they appear on the screen. (The steps are described later in this entry.) Excel inserts the chart sheet into the active workbook, just to the left of the active worksheet.

shortcut

Select the range of data on the active worksheet and then position the mouse pointer over the sheet tab at the bottom of the workbook. Click the right mouse button to view the shortcut menu for the sheet. Choose **Insert**. In the resulting **Insert** dialog box, select **Chart** and click OK. The first **ChartWizard** dialog box appears on the screen.

To Create an Embedded Chart from a Chart Sheet

1. Activate the chart sheet and choose **Edit** ➢ **Copy** (or press **Ctrl-C**). A moving border appears around the chart.

2. Activate the worksheet where you want to copy the chart object, and select the worksheet location where you want to place the embedded chart.

3. Choose **Edit** ➢ **Paste** (or press **Ctrl-V**).

ChartWizard

The ChartWizard is Excel's step-by-step guide through the process of creating an embedded chart. Using the ChartWizard you can easily make specific decisions about the type, format, and structure of your chart, and about the link between the

16

chart and the source data. You can also add elements such as a title, axis labels, and a legend during the ChartWizard procedure. Many Excel users find the ChartWizard the most efficient and effective way to create charts.

To Use the ChartWizard

1. On the source worksheet, select the data from which you want to create a chart. In the range selection you can include a first row and a first column of labels that describe or identify the numeric data.

2. Click the **ChartWizard** button in the Standard toolbar. Then drag the mouse pointer over the worksheet area where you want to display the chart you are about to create. When you release the mouse button, Excel displays the first of five dialog boxes, this one named **ChartWizard - Step 1 of 5**.

3. In the first dialog box. you can change or confirm the source data range for the chart. If the reference displayed in the **Range** box is correct, click the **Next** button.

4. In the second ChartWizard dialog box, Excel displays icons representing the available chart types. Select one of these icons and click the **Next** button.

5. In the third dialog box, Excel displays icons representing a variety of formats for the chart type you have selected. Select a format and click **Next** to continue.

6. In the fourth ChartWizard dialog box, you make decisions that will affect the link between the worksheet data and the chart. First, select **Rows** or **Columns** to specify whether the data series for the chart should be read from the rows or the columns of the source data table. Then specify whether the first column and first row of the data table contain entries that should be used as labels or as data points in the chart. Study the **Sample**

Chart box to see if the resulting chart is the one you want to create. Click **Next** to continue.

7. Finally, the fifth dialog box gives you options for including a legend, a chart title, and axis titles. Enter the titles in the appropriate text boxes, and study the sample chart to confirm that your entries are correct.

8. Click **Finish**. Excel creates a chart on your worksheet, following the specifications you have supplied in the five ChartWizard dialog boxes.

 tip

You can use the **Back** button in the ChartWizard dialog boxes to backtrack to the previous dialog box.

Clearing Data

Excel gives you several simple techniques for erasing data from a range of worksheet cells, and for clearing any format options you have applied to the range.

To Clear Data with the Clear Command

1. Select the range of worksheet data that you want to delete.

2. Choose **Edit ➢ Clear**.

3. Select one of the four options in the **Clear** submenu: **All**, to delete all entries, formats, and notes; **Formats**, to delete formatting only; **Contents**, to delete text, numbers, and formula entries; or **Notes** to delete any notes you have entered in the worksheet range.

4. Click **OK** to complete the clear operation.

18

 **techno note**

A *note* is a text annotation that you attach to a cell. To create or view a note, you choose **Insert ➢ Note**. Notice that you can select either **All** or **Notes** in the **Clear** submenu to erase notes from a cell or range.

 shortcut

To clear the contents of a selected range you can simply press the Del key. Alternatively, click the right mouse button and choose **Clear Contents** from the shortcut menu.

 reminder

To undo an inadvertent clear operation, select **Edit ➢ Undo Clear** (or press Ctrl-Z) *immediately* after the clear. See *Undo* on page 116 for more information.

To Use the Dragging Technique for Clearing Data

1. Select the range of data that you want to clear.

2. Position the mouse pointer over the fill handle, the small black square located at the lower-right corner of the selection. The mouse pointer is displayed as a cross-hair shape.

3. Drag the fill handle up or to the left, over the data that you want to delete. The range that you drag over is displayed in gray.

4. Release the mouse button. Excel clears the data from the range.

tip

If you want to delete data, formats, and notes, hold down **Ctrl** while you drag back over the range.

warning

When you clear data from a range, the column widths and row heights in the range remain unchanged.

Colors

Several formatting commands in Excel provide color palettes or color lists from which you can select the display colors for worksheets and charts.

For worksheets, the color selections appear in the **Font**, **Patterns**, and **Border** tabs of the **Format Cells** dialog box (choose **Format ➤ Cells**).

For charts, color selections are available on the **Patterns** tab (and where appropriate, the **Font** tab) of the **Format ➤ Selected** commands—for example, Format ➤ Selected Chart **Area**, **Format ➤ Selected Plot Area**, **Format ➤ Selected Series**, and so on. This menu changes to reflect the part of the chart currently selected. Alternatively, you can double-click on the area of the chart you wish to format and the appropriate dialog box will appear.

20

Excel 5 provides some convenient shortcuts for selecting colors. The **Color** and **Font Color** buttons on the **Formatting** toolbar provide color palettes with large selections of colors. These are "tear-off" palettes that you can drag into the Excel work area and use for making several color changes in sequence.

To Display Worksheet Entries in Color

1. Select the range of worksheet data that you want to display in color.

2. Choose **Format** ➢ **Cells** and click the **Font** tab in the **Format Cells** dialog box.

3. Click the arrow at the right side of the **Color** box to view the selection of colors available for displaying data.

4. Select a color and click **OK**.

warning

When you select a range on the worksheet, the colors change due to the selection highlight. To view the true colors, deselect the range.

To Change the Cell Color of a Range

1. Select the worksheet range where you want to apply a new color.

2. Choose **Format** ➢ **Cells** and click the **Patterns** tab in the **Format Cells** dialog box.

3. Select a color in the **Color** palette.

4. Optionally, click the down-arrow next to the **Pattern** box and make a new selection in the resulting palette. The Sample box shows what your combined color and pattern selections will look like.

5. Click **OK** to apply these selections to the current range.

 reminder

A non-solid pattern consists of a combination of foreground and background colors. When you select the solid pattern, only the foreground color applies—in other words, the solid color fills the area behind any entry in the cell. See *Patterns* on page 88 for more information.

To Change the Border Color in a Worksheet Selection

I. Select the worksheet range where you want to change the border color.

2. Choose **Format** ➢ **Cells** and click the **Border** tab.

3. Select a border location and style. (See *Borders* on page 7 for details.)

4. Click the arrow at the right of the **Color** box and select a color for the border. Click **OK**.

 shortcut

Select a range, click the right mouse button, and choose **Format Cells** from the shortcut menu.

22

To Change the Color of a Chart Area or Chart Item

1. In a chart, select the area or item that you want to change.

2. Choose **Format ➤ Selected ...**. (The name of this command corresponds to the object you've selected in the chart.)

3. Click the **Patterns** tab and choose a color from the **Area** colors.

4. If the object you've selected contains text, click the **Font** tab and make a selection from the **Color** list.

5. Click OK.

Column Width

By adjusting the widths of selected columns in a worksheet, you can display large amounts of data as clearly and effectively as possible.

To Change the Width of a Single Column

1. Select a cell in the column, or click the column heading to select the entire column.

2. Choose **Format ➤ Column** and then choose **Width** from the submenu.

3. Enter a new value in the **Column Width** text box. Then click **OK**.

techno note

The value in the **Column Width** box is the width of the column in characters, given the current font and point size. The

standard column width for a worksheet is the width of all columns
that you have not adjusted individually. To change the standard
width setting, choose **Format** ➢ **Column** and click **Standard
Width** in the resulting submenu. Then enter a new value in
the **Standard Width** text box.

shortcut

To use a visual technique for adjusting the width of a column,
position the mouse pointer over the line located just to the
right of the column's heading. Drag the line to the right (for a
wider column) or to the left (for a narrower column).

recommended

To find the *best* fit for the contents of a given column, double-
click the line located just to the right of the column's heading.

tip

To change the widths of a group of columns, select the columns and choose **Format** ➢ **Column** ➢ **Width**.

Copying Data

Like all major Windows applications, Excel provides the familiar
Copy and **Paste** commands for copying data from one place to
another. These commands use the Clipboard to complete the

copy operation. In addition, Excel has a simple drag-and-drop procedure that you can use to copy a range of data.

To Copy Data Using Copy and Paste

1. Select the range of data that you want to copy.

2. Choose **Edit** ➢ **Copy**. Excel displays a moving border around the range, and copies the data to the Clipboard.

3. Select a cell or range for the destination. (If you select a single cell, it becomes the upper-left corner of the copied data.)

4. Choose **Edit** ➢ **Paste**. Excel copies the data to the target range.

 shortcut

To copy the selected data to the Clipboard, press **Ctrl-C**. To paste the data, press **Ctrl-V**. Note that the **Copy** and **Paste** commands are also available on the shortcut menu for work-sheet cells. (See *Shortcut Menus* on page 111.)

 warning

If you select a paste area that already contains data, the **Paste** command overwrites the previous data entries with the copied data. (See *Inserting* on page 65 to learn how to avoid this problem.)

To Copy a Selection to Multiple Locations

1. Select the range of data that you want to copy.

2. Choose **Edit** ➢ **Copy** or press **Ctrl+C**.

3. Select the first range to which you want to copy the data. Then hold down **Ctrl** as you select each additional range.

4. Choose **Edit** ➢ **Paste** or press **Ctrl+V**. Excel copies the data to all of the selected ranges at once.

To Copy Data Using Drag-and-Drop

1. Select the range of data that you want to copy.

2. Position the mouse pointer along the border of the selection. The pointer shape changes to a white arrow.

3. Hold down **Ctrl** and drag the mouse pointer to the location where you want to copy the data. A small plus sign appears next to the arrow pointer when you hold down **Ctrl**. A gray frame representing the copy area follows the mouse pointer as you drag.

4. Release the mouse button, then release **Ctrl**. Excel copies the data from the copy range to the paste range.

Copying Formats

Once you have formatted a range of worksheet data in just the way you want it, you may want to copy the same formatting options to another range. To do so you can use either **Edit** ➢ **Paste Special** or the **Format Painter** button in the Standard toolbar.

reminder

The formats you copy from one range to another include options selected from several commands in the Format menu—
options such as alignments, fonts, borders, and patterns and
number formats.

To Copy Formats
from One Range to Another

1. Select the range from which you want to copy formatting options.

2. Choose **Edit** ➤ **Copy**. A moving border appears around
the copy range.

3. Select a cell or range to which you want to copy the
formatting from the copy range.

4. Choose **Edit** ➤ **Paste Special**.

5. In the **Paste Special** dialog box, select the **Formats**
option and click **OK**. In response, Excel applies all
the formats from the copy range to the paste range.

To Copy Formats
Using the Format Painter Button

1. Select the range that contains the formats you want
to copy.

2. Click the **Format Painter** button in the Standard toolbar. When you move the mouse pointer into the
worksheet area, the pointer appears as a cross with a
paintbrush icon.

3. Select the area that you want to format, or simply click the upper-left corner cell of the area. Excel copies the formats from the source range to the destination.

Copying Formulas

When you copy a formula from one location to another in a worksheet, the result depends upon the types of references you have included in the original formula: An *absolute reference* is copied verbatim from the original formula to the copy; each copy refers to a fixed location on the worksheet. A *relative reference* is adjusted according to the location of the copy, so that the row and/or column portions of the reference may be different for each copy of the formula. A *mixed reference* contains a mixture of absolute and relative elements. You can use copy-and-paste, AutoFill, or drag-and-drop operations to copy formulas from one location to another. In addition, you can use **Edit** ➤ **Paste Special** to convert all the formulas in a range to fixed values.

 reminder

See *References* on page 96 for more information about reference types in Excel.

To Create and Copy a Formula

1. While you enter the first copy of a formula, decide whether each reference should be absolute, relative, or mixed—depending on how you want the reference to be copied across rows and/or down columns. Enter a reference into the formula bar (by pointing with the mouse or by typing the reference directly from the keyboard), and then press F4 repeatedly to step through the possible reference types: relative, absolute, mixed. Excel inserts a dollar sign ($) before the absolute portions of the reference.

2. After you complete the original formula, use any of the techniques available in Excel for copying an entry from one location to another. (See *Copying Data* on page 24 for the steps of these various techniques.)

For example, consider the following formula, which contains two mixed references and one absolute reference:

```
=(B$4+$B5)*$B$1
```

Suppose you enter this formula into cell C5 of a worksheet. If you then copy the formula down column C to cells C6 and C7, the first mixed reference (B$4) is copied unchanged, but the row portion of the second mixed reference ($B5) is adjusted in each copy:

```
C6=(B$4+$B6)*$B$1
C7=(B$4+$B7)*$B$1
```

Conversely, if you copy the formula across row 5 to cells D5 and E5, the first reference is adjusted but the second reference remains unchanged in each copy:

```
D5                    E5
=(C$4+$B5)*$B$1  =(D$4+$B5)*$B$1
```

Notice that the absolute reference, B1, remains unchanged in all copies of the formula.

To Convert Formulas to Fixed Values in a Worksheet Range

1. Select the range of cells containing the formulas you want to convert.

2. Choose **Edit** ➢ **Copy**.

3. Without changing the range selection, select **Edit** ➢ **Paste Special**.

4. In the **Paste Special** dialog box, choose the **Values** option and click **OK**. Excel converts each formula entry in the range to its current value. In other words, the range now contains only constant entries and the background formulas are lost.

tip

To restore the background formulas, choose **Edit** ➢ **Undo Paste Special** (or press **Ctrl-Z**) immediately after this operation.

shortcut

To convert a formula in the formula bar to its current value, press the **F9** function key while the formula bar is active.

Data Form

A data form is a dialog box designed to simplify your work with lists and databases in Excel. A list is a collection of data arranged in rows and columns, where the top row contains a label for each column of data. You can think of a list as a *database*, where each row is a record, each column a field, and the top row contains field names. See *Database* on page 36 and *Lists* on page 72 for more information.

You use a data form to examine and edit the fields of individual records, to scroll through the list one record at a time, to add new records to the list, to delete records from the list, and to search for records that match specific criteria.

To Use a Data Form for Viewing Records

1. Open or activate a worksheet that contains a list. Select any cell within the range of the list.

2. Choose **Data ➤ Form**. The data form for the current list appears on the screen. At the left side of the form are labels identifying the fields of the list, and text boxes showing the field entries for the first record. At the right side is a column of command buttons you can use to perform specific operations on your list.

3. Use the vertical scroll bar in the middle of the data form to scroll one record at a time through the list, or to move quickly from one position to another in the database. At the upper-right corner of the data form, Excel displays the current record number and the total number of records; for example, 5 *of* 10.

4. Click the **Close** button to close the data form when you are finished viewing records of the database.

warning

Excel displays a maximum of 32 fields in a data form. If your list contains more fields than this, the **Data** ➤ **Form** command displays an error message: *Too many fields in the data form.*

To Edit a Record in the Data Form

1. Choose **Data** ➤ **Form** to open the data form for the current list.

2. Scroll to the record that you want to edit, and make changes in any of the text boxes displaying the fields of the record.

3. Scroll to a different record. As soon as you do so, Excel copies the changes in the edited record to the database itself.

tip

Before scrolling to a different record, you can click the **Restore** button to bring back the original unedited version of the current record. Once you scroll to a different record, however, any changes you have made are copied to the database.

techno note

Calculated fields cannot be edited in the data form. (You create a calculated field by entering a formula as the first entry in a given field, and copying the formula down the field's column.) The data form displays the current value of each calculated field, but not in a text box.

32

To Add New Records
to the Database in the Data Form

1. Choose **Data ➤ Form** to open the data form for the current list.

2. Click the **New** button. The data form displays blank text boxes for all of the fields that can be edited. The words *New Record* appear at the upper-right corner of the data form.

3. Enter a data item for each of the fields of the new record. (Press **Tab** to move from one field to another.)

4. Press ↵ to add the new record to the list. The data form displays blank fields for the next new record.

5. Repeat steps 3 and 4 for each new record you want to add to the list.

6. Click the **Close** button to close the data form.

 tip

The data form always appends new records to the end of the list, regardless of the current order of other records. Choose **Data ➤ Sort** to rearrange the list after you have added one or more records. (See *Sorting* on page 112.)

 **techno note**

If your list contains one or more computed fields, Excel automatically copies the formulas into each new record that you add into the data form.

To Delete a Record in the Data Form

1. Choose **Data ➤ Form** to open the data form for the current list.

2. Scroll to the record that you want to delete.

3. Click the **Delete** button. A message box appears on the screen, asking you to confirm the deletion.

4. Click **OK** to delete the record from the list, or click **Cancel** to back out of the deletion.

 warning

You cannot undo a record deletion that you complete in the data form. By contrast, if you delete a record by deleting its row directly from the worksheet (select the row and choose **Edit ➤ Delete**), you can choose **Edit ➤ Undo Delete** to bring back the record.

To Search for Records in the Data Form

1. Choose **Data ➤ Form** to open the data form for the current list.

2. Click the **Criteria** button. The data form displays a blank text box for each of the fields in the list, including the calculated fields. The word *Criteria* appears in the upper-right corner of the data form, and the scroll bar is temporarily removed.

3. Enter a comparison criterion into any one of the field boxes. The criterion can be any text or numeric entry that you want to search for. Alternatively, you can

34

begin the criterion expression with any of Excel's six comparison operators (=, <, >, <=, >=, <>), or you can include wildcard characters (* or ?) to search for variations of matching text. (See *Database Criteria* on page 37 for more information about criteria expressions.)

4. Repeat step 3 for each field in which you want to include a criterion. If you enter multiple criteria into the data form, Excel reads them as "and" conditions. This means that a record must meet all of the criteria to be selected as a match.

5. Click the **Find Next** button to find the first record that matches your criteria, and then click the same button repeatedly to find other matching records. Optionally, click the **Find Prev** button to scroll backwards through the matching records. Excel beeps in response to either button when there are no more matching records in the specified direction.

6. Click **Close** to close the data form when you are finished examining the matching records.

 tip

You can revise the search criteria at any time while the data form is open. Click the **Criteria** button to view the current criteria, and edit the entry in any of the field boxes. Click **Clear** to erase all the current criteria, or click **Restore** to bring back the previous criteria.

warning

Excel does not retain the criteria when you close the data form. The next time you open the data form and click the **Criteria** button, all of the field boxes will be blank.

Database

A *database* is a rectangular arrangement of information stored in a worksheet. The columns in the database range are known as fields, and the rows are records. The top row of the database contains the field names.

In the vocabulary of Excel 5, a database is one kind of list you can create to keep records in a worksheet. After you create a list—whether you think of your list as a database or not—you can perform a variety of operations, such as searching for records that match specified criteria, copying selected records to a new location, and sorting the database. See Lists on page 72 for information about these operations. In addition, Excel provides a special data form dialog box that simplifies several basic database operations. See Data Form on page 30 for details.

To Create an Excel Database

1. In a worksheet, enter a row of field names at the top of the range where you plan to create the database. Enter a unique field name in each cell.

2. Use a formatting option of your choice to give the field names a distinctive appearance from the rest of the database. For example, select the row of field names and click the **Bold** button on the **Formatting** toolbar.

3. Enter one record of information in each row after the
field names. A field entry may be text, a number, a
date, a time value, or even a formula, but the entries in
a given field column should all contain the same type
of data. Do not leave any rows blank between records.

 tip

A field name is any text entry. In writing field names you do
not necessarily have to follow the same rules that Excel imposes
on range names. But some database operations are simplified
if field names are written as legal range names. (See *Names* on
page 76 for information about range names.)

Database Criteria

To perform operations on a selection of records in a database,
you create a *criteria range*. Excel uses the expressions in this
range to determine whether a given record matches your selection criteria. In the criteria range, you can write *comparison
criteria* to find records that contain a certain value or a range of
values; or *computed criteria* to find records based on a formula.
Once you have created a criteria range, you can use Excel's
database commands to find, extract, or delete matching records.

Creating a criteria range is a database technique that has been
available in all versions of Excel. In Excel 5, a new technique
known as AutoFilter can often simplify your work with lists
and databases. (See *Filters* on page 46 and *Lists* on page 72 .)

To Create a Criteria Range

1. Select a location in the rows *above* your database. (Insert the rows if necessary, using **Insert ➢ Rows**. Note that a criteria range located in the rows beneath the database range might limit the growth of the database itself. A criteria range next to the database might be hidden when the database is filtered.)

2. Enter a row of field names for the criteria range. The row may contain all of the field names from the database or only a selection of names. (For a computed criterion, enter a name that is not the same as any field name in the database.)

3. In the row or rows beneath the field names, enter the criteria expressions.

 **techno note**

Within the criteria range, you can enter a single expression or multiple expressions. Excel's interpretation of your criteria depends on how you arrange the expressions in the rows and columns of the criteria range. Multiple criteria in the same row result in an "and" condition—that is, a record must match *all* the criteria in the row to be selected. Multiple criteria in a column result in an "or" condition; a record may be selected if it matches *any one* of the expressions in a given column.

 tip

A comparison criterion consists of a simple text or numeric entry, or an expression that begins with one of Excel's six comparison operators: =, <, >, <=, >=, or <>.

38

A computed criterion is a formula that includes a relative reference to at least one of the fields in the database. The reference may appear as a field name, whether or not you have actually defined field names as range names in your worksheet. For example, in an inventory database you might use the computed criterion =Quantity<=Reorder to find all the records in which the quantity on hand is less than the amount specified as the reorder point. In other words, you would use this criterion to find items that need to be reordered. Keep in mind that the name for a computed criterion—that is, the name you enter above the criterion in the criteria range—should not be the same as any of the field names.

Date and Time Entries

You can enter a date or time value into a worksheet cell in any of several formats that Excel recognizes. In response, Excel applies a predefined date or time format to the cell. Internally, the entry itself is stored as a special type of numeric value known as a *serial number*. The serial number allows you to perform *date and time arithmetic* in a worksheet.

To Enter a Date or Time Value into a Worksheet Cell

Select the cell and enter the value in a date or time format that Excel recognizes.

Here are some examples of date formats that Excel accepts as entries in a worksheet:

> 3/14/94
>
> 3-14-94

March 14, 1994

14 Mar 1994

In response to these entries, Excel applies one of its predefined date formats to the cell—displaying the date either as 3/14/94 or 14-Mar-94. Excel stores the date internally as 34407, which is the serial number for March 14, 1994.

Here are some examples of time formats that Excel accepts as entries into a worksheet:

6:00

6 AM

6:00 AM

6:00:00 AM

In response to any of these entries, Excel applies one of its predefined time formats to the cell—displaying the time as 6:00 or 6:00 AM or 6:00:00 AM. Excel stores the time internally as the serial number 0.25, signifying that one-fourth of the day is over at 6:00 AM.

 tip

The starting date of Excel's serial number system is January 1, 1900; this date has a serial number of 1. The last date in the system is December 31, 2078, which has a serial number of 65380.

A full serial number contain digits both before and after the decimal point. In this case, the integer portion before the decimal point represents the date, and the fractional value after the decimal point represents the time. (Specifically, the fraction is the portion of the day that has elapsed at a given time.)

For example, 34407.25 represents the date/time value March 14, 1994 6:00 AM.

To Find the Difference between Two Dates in a Worksheet

Enter a formula that subtracts one date entry from another. For example, suppose you have entered date values in cells B1 and C1. The following formula gives the difference between the two values:

    =C1–B1

Internally, Excel subtracts one serial number from the other. The result is the difference in days between the two dates.

 tip

To include a literal date in a formula, enclose the date in double quotation marks and use a date format that Excel recognizes. For example, the formula ="3/14/94"+90 adds 90 days to the date 3/14/94. The result is the serial number equivalent of the date 6/12/94.

To display a serial number in an equivalent date format, choose **Format ➤ Cells** and click the **Number** tab. Select the **Date** category, select a date format, and click **OK**. (See *Number Formats* on page 80 for more information.)

 **shortcut**

Use the keyboard shortcut **Ctrl+Shift+3** to display a selected serial number entry as a date.

To Find the Difference between Two Time Entries in a Worksheet

Enter a formula that subtracts one time from the other and multiplies the difference by 24. The result is the difference in hours between the two time entries. For example, suppose you have entered time values in cells B1 and C1. The following formula gives the difference in hours between the two values:

```
=(C1–B1)*24
```

Deleting

You can use either the **Delete** command or a special mouse technique to delete rows, columns, or a selection of cells from a worksheet. When you do so, Excel shifts other cells up or to the left to fill in the deleted area.

 reminder

Keep in mind the distinction between *clearing data* from a range and *deleting* a range. The **Clear** command erases the contents of a range, but leaves the range itself intact. By contrast, the **Delete** command removes a range completely and shifts the neighboring cells to take its place. (See *Clearing Data* on page 18 for more information.)

To Delete Entire Rows or Columns

1. Select the rows or columns by dragging the mouse along the appropriate row headings or column headings. (To select a single row or column, click the row heading or the column heading.)

2. Choose **Edit** ➢ **Delete**.

 shortcut

Excel provides a convenient mouse technique as a visual alternative to **Edit** ➢ **Delete**. Select the group of rows or columns that you want to delete. Then hold down **Shift** and drag the fill handle up (to delete rows) or to the left (to delete columns). Excel highlights the selection in gray. Release the mouse button and then **Shift** to complete the deletion.

When you select entire rows, the fill handle is located at the lower-left corner of the selection. When you select entire columns, the fill handle is at the upper-right corner of the selection.

 tip

To undo a deletion, choose **Edit** ➢ **Undo Delete** (or press **Ctrl+Z**) immediately after the deletion.

To Delete a Range of Cells

1. Select the range you want to delete.

2. Select **Edit** ➢ **Delete**.

3. On the **Delete** dialog box, select the **Shift Cells Left** or **Shift Cells Up** option, depending how you want Excel to fill in the empty area.

4. Click OK.

 shortcut

Again, a visual mouse technique is available. Select the range that you want to delete. Then hold down **Shift**, and drag the fill handle left to shift cells left, or up to shift cells up. No dialog box appears.

Exiting Excel

When you close its application window, Excel reminds you to save any worksheets or other documents that you have changed but not updated.

To Exit Excel

Choose **File ➢ Exit**. For each unsaved document, Excel displays a prompt asking you for instructions: Click **Yes** to save the document to disk, or click **No** to abandon the changes in the document. Click **Cancel** to return to the Excel application window.

 shortcut

Press **Alt+F4**, or double-click the control menu box at the left side of the Excel window's title bar.

Filling Ranges

The **Edit ➢ Fill** commands are designed to fill a range of cells by copying the contents of a single cell located at the beginning or end of the range. Alternatively, you can fill all the cells of a range by selecting the range before you begin an entry.

To Use the Edit ➢ Fill Commands to Copy Entries

1. Enter a number, text entry, or formula into the beginning or ending cell of the range you want to fill. Optionally, apply formats to the entry.

2. Starting from the cell containing the entry, select the row or column range that you want to fill.

3. Choose **Edit ➢ Fill**. From the **Fill** submenu, choose **Right** or **Left** to fill a row, or **Down** or **Up** to fill a column. Excel copies the entry and formats in the first or last cell to all the cells in the range.

 shortcut

Press **Ctrl-R** to fill a row to the right, or **Ctrl-D** to fill a column down.

Alternatively, the fill handle is often the best tool to use for filling a range of cells. See *AutoFill* on page 4 for details.

 note

You can use the **Edit ➢ Fill** commands to fill multiple rows or columns at once. To fill rows, select a range in which the first

45

or last column contains the data you want to copy, choose **Edit ➤ Fill**, and click **Right** or **Left**. To fill columns, select a range in which the first or last row contains the data, choose **Edit ➤ Fill**, and click the **Down** or **Up**. A fill operation overwrites any existing data in the range of the fill.

To Enter Data or Formulas into an Entire Range at Once

1. Select the range into which you want to enter the data or formulas.

2. Type the entry into the formula bar.

3. Press **Ctrl-↵** to complete the entry. Excel copies the entry into each cell of the range.

warning

Do not confuse the **Ctrl+↵** shortcut with **Ctrl+Shift+↵**, which defines an *array* in the selected range

Filters

Filters allow you to work with selected rows of information in any list, including a list that you have organized as a database. (See *Database* on page 36 and *Lists* on page 72 for background information.)

Excel 5 gives you two effective ways to filter a list or database. The simpler of the two techniques is known as AutoFilter. When you select this feature, Excel provides drop-down lists at the top of every column in your database; you can quickly filter the database by selecting entries in one or more of the drop-down lists.

The second technique, known as Advanced Filter, makes use of a *criteria range* that you create for your database. The criteria range contains values or expressions Excel can use to select records from your database. (See *Database Criteria* on page 37 for details.) Using the Advanced Filter command, you can temporarily hide records that do not match your criteria, or you can copy matching records to a new location.

To Filter a List or Database with AutoFilter

1. Activate the worksheet that contains your list or database, and select any cell within the range of data.

2. Choose **Data** ➤ **Filter** and then choose **AutoFilter** from the Filter submenu. In response, Excel displays drop-down arrows in the first row of your database, where the field names are located.

3. Click the drop-down arrow at the top of any column. The resulting list shows all the unique data entries in the column, along with several other options. Select an entry. Excel immediately hides all the records that do not match your selection.

4. Repeat step 3 in other columns to apply additional filters to your database. To be displayed in the filtered database, a record must match *all* of the selections that you make in the drop-down lists.

Figure 3 shows what a database looks like after you have chosen the AutoFilter. In the top row of the database, a drop-down arrow appears next to each field name. As shown in the Specialty field, the resulting drop-down list contains all the unique data entries in the field, along with other options.

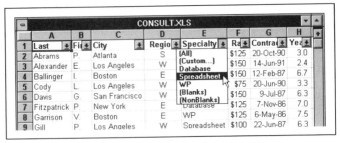

FIGURE 3: The effect of the AutoFilter command

 tip

In addition to the unique data entries in a given column, each drop-down list contains four additional options that you can use for special purposes:

- ⊙ Choose **(All)** to view all the data in the current column. (Filters in other columns remain in effect.)

- ⊙ Choose **(Custom...)** to apply complex or compound criteria to your database. (See the instructions in the next part of this entry.)

- ⊙ Choose **(Blanks)** to display only those records that contain blank cells in the current column.

- ⊙ Choose **(NonBlanks)** to display only those records that contain nonblank entries in the current column.

To Apply Custom Criteria to a Filtered Database

1. Select a cell in the database, choose **Data ➢ Filter** and then choose **AutoFilter**. Drop-down arrows appear at the top of the database.

2. Click any drop-down arrow and choose the **(Custom...)** entry. The **Custom AutoFilter** dialog box appears on the screen. It contains four boxes in which you can develop one or two criteria to apply to the current column. Each criterion consists of a *relational operator* selection and a data selection.

3. Click the drop-down arrow next to the first relational operator box. Select one of the six operators in the resulting list: =, >, <, >=, <=, or <>.

4. Click the drop-down arrow for the adjacent box. The list contains all the unique data entries in the current column. Select an entry to complete the criterion. (Alternatively, enter a new value into this box—a value that does not necessarily appear in the database column.)

5. Optionally, repeat steps 3 and 4 to develop another criterion in the second row of text boxes. If you do so, you must select either the **And** or the **Or** option button to connect the two criteria. The **And** option means that a record must match *both* criteria to be selected. The **Or** option means that a record will be selected if it matches one or both criteria.

6. Click the **OK** button to apply the custom criteria you have developed. In response, Excel hides all records that do not match your criteria.

 tip

To apply a filter consisting of more than two criteria, create a criteria range and use the **Advanced Filter**. (See the details below.)

To Display all the Records in a Filtered List or Database

Choose **Data** ➤ **Filter** and then choose **Show All** from the **Filter** submenu. In response, Excel redisplays all the hidden records in the database.

To Remove a Filter from a List or Database

Choose **Data** ➤ **Filter** and then choose **AutoFilter** from the **Filter** submenu so that the check mark is removed. Excel removes the drop-down arrows from the top of the database, and redisplays any hidden records.

To Use a Criteria Range to Filter a Database

1. Develop a criteria range in the rows above your database, as described in *Database Criteria* on page 37.

2. Select any cell within the database range.

3. Select **Data** ➤ **Filter** and click the **Advanced Filter** command. In the **List Range** text box of the **Advanced Filter** dialog box, Excel automatically enters the range of your database.

4. Activate the **Criteria Range** text box, and enter a reference to the criteria range you have developed on the worksheet. (Alternatively, use the mouse to point to the range.)

5. Make sure that the default **Filter** option is selected in the **Action** group, and click OK. Excel filters the database in place, temporarily hiding all records that do not match the criteria you have expressed in the criteria range.

Finding Worksheet Data

You can use the **Edit ➢ Find** command to search for a sequence of text in the entries of a worksheet.

To Search for Data in a Worksheet

1. Activate the worksheet in which you want to perform the search, and choose **Edit ➢ Find**. The **Find** dialog box appears on the screen.

2. In the **Find What** box, enter the text that you want to search for.

3. In the **Search** box, select **By Rows** to search from the top to the bottom of your worksheet, or **By Columns** to search from left to right.

4. In the **Look in** box, select the kind of cell contents that you want to search through: **Formulas**, **Values**, or **Notes**.

5. Click the **Match Case** option, placing an X in its check box, if you want Excel to search for the text in the exact uppercase and lowercase combinations you entered into the **Find What** box. Leave this option unchecked if you want to perform the search without regard for alphabetic case.

6. Click the **Find Entire Cells Only** option, placing an X in its check box, if the text you have entered in the **Find What** box represents an entire cell entry. Leave this option unchecked if you want to search for the text as a portion of a cell entry.

7. Click the **Find Next** button to begin the search.

shortcut

Press **Shift+F5** to open the **Find** dialog box.

warning

If Excel does not find the target text in your worksheet, a dialog box appears on the screen with the message *Cannot find
matching data*. If the search is unsuccessful, but you believe the
text does exist in your worksheet, reopen the **Find** dialog box
and make sure you have selected appropriate options in the
Look in and **Search** boxes.

a better way

You can use wildcard characters in the search text: **?** stands for
a single unspecified character, and ***** stands for a string of unspecified characters.

Fonts

You can display and print worksheet data in any of the fonts
available in your installation of Windows. You can also select a
type size and any combination of styles—including bold, italics, underlining, and others. In addition, Excel 5 allows "rich
text" formatting; this means that you can apply different formats to individual characters within a text entry in a cell.

To Change the Font of a Selection

1. Select a range of cells, choose **Format ➤ Cells** and click on the **Font** tab. The resulting dialog box has **Font**, **Font Style**, **Size**, **Underline**, **Effects**, and **Color** options.

2. Select a font name from the **Font** box, and a numeric setting from the **Size** box.

3. Select any of the **Font Style** options: **Regular**, **Italic**, **Bold**, **Bold Italic**. Optionally select the **Underline** option and click any of the check boxes in the **Effects** box.

4. Click **OK** to apply the font to the current selection.

shortcut

Press **Ctrl+B**, **Ctrl+I**, or **Ctrl+U** to apply bold, italics, or underlining to a selected cell or range. You can also click the arrow button to the right of the **Font** text box in the Formatting toolbar to view the list of fonts you can apply to selected text.

tip

As you select options in the **Font** dialog box, the **Sample** box shows what the resulting text will look like. To undo all selections and return to the *normal* font, place an X in the **Normal Font** check box. The normal font is the default for a given worksheet.

To Apply Fonts and Styles to Individual Characters in a Text Entry

1. Double-click the cell that contains the text entry. A flashing insertion bar appears at the end of the entry in its cell, indicating that you can now edit the text.

2. Use the mouse or the keyboard to highlight the characters whose font or style you want to change.

3. Click buttons in the Formatting toolbar to make changes in the selected text—for example, click the Bold, Italic, or Underline buttons, or make a selection from the Font Color palette. Alternatively, choose Format ➢ Cells, make selections from the Font, Style, Size, Underline, Color, or Effects options, and click OK.

4. Optionally, repeat steps 2 and 3 to change the formatting of other character selections within the text entry.

5. Press Enter to confirm the changes.

 shortcut

You can also format the characters of a text entry while you are first typing the entry, just as you would in word-processed text. One easy way to do this is to use keyboard shortcuts such as Ctrl-B, Ctrl-I, and Ctrl-U to switch into and out of specific formatting effects—in this case, boldface, italics, and underlining.

To Change the Default Font for all the Worksheets in a Workbook

1. Activate the workbook, and choose **Format ➢ Style**. The **Style** dialog box appears on the screen.

2. In the **Style Name** list, choose **Normal** if it is not already the selection.

3. Click the **Modify** button. The **Format Cells** dialog box appears on the screen. Click the **Font** tab.

4. Choose any combination of font settings in the resulting **Font** dialog box, and then click **OK**.

5. Click **OK** in the **Style** dialog box. The font selection is now the default for the active workbook.

Formatting Worksheet Cells

You can change the appearance of data in a worksheet by applying formats to selected cells or ranges. Excel's formatting options include varieties of numeric display formats, alignments, fonts, borders, and patterns.

To Change the Format of a Range of Cells

Select the range, choose **Format ➤ Cells**. Click one of the following tabs in the resulting dialog box:

- **Number** changes the display format of numeric values in the range. (See *Number Formats* on page 80 for details.)

- **Alignment** determines the horizontal and vertical alignment, and the orientation of individual data entries in their cells. (See *Alignment* on page 1.)

- **Font** provides a variety of fonts, sizes, styles, and display colors for the data in a range. (See *Fonts* on page 52.)

- **Border** displays borders in several styles along selected sides of cells in a range. (See *Borders* on page 7.)

- **Patterns** changes the background pattern and color of a range of cells. (See *Patterns* on page 88.)

- **Protection** changes the protection scheme of locked cells and/or hidden formulas.

To Change the Default Formats for an Entire Worksheet

Choose the **Format** ➤ **Style** and click **Modify** to change the definition of the worksheet's Normal style. (See *Fonts* on page 52 for an example.)

Formula Bar

The formula bar is the line just above the work area in the Excel window. You can use the formula bar to enter or edit data. Excel 5 also allows you to edit an entry directly in the cell where it is stored.

To Enter Text or a Numeric Value into a Worksheet Cell

1. Select the cell and begin typing the entry. Your entry appears on the formula bar. The active formula bar also displays an enter box (a check-mark icon), a cancel box (an X icon) and a Function Wizard button.

2. When you finish typing the entry, press ↵ or click the enter box to complete the entry.

 reminder

To cancel an entry without changing the contents of the current cell, click the cancel box, or press **Esc**.

To Edit the Current Entry in a Cell

Select the cell and press **F2** to activate the formula bar or click the mouse inside the formula bar. Alternatively, double-click the cell whose contents you want to edit. You can edit the contents either in the formula bar or in the cell itself.

 tip

In the **Edit** mode, press **Home** or ↑ to move the insertion point to the beginning of the formula bar. Press **End** or ↓ to move to the end of the current entry. Press ← or → to move the insertion point left or right by one character.

Formulas

A formula in Excel is an entry that performs a calculation or other operation on one or more operands. A formula begins with an equal sign (=) and may include values, references, names, functions, and operations. The formula's result is displayed in the cell where you enter the formula. The formula itself appears in the formula bar when you select the cell.

To Enter a Formula into a Cell

1. Type = to begin the formula
2. Enter an *operand*, such as a number, a text or date entry (enclosed in quotes), or a reference to a cell that contains a data item.
3. Optionally, enter an arithmetic operator (+, -, *, /, ^, or %), a comparison operator (<, >, ≤, ≥, <>, or =) or a text operator (&).

4. Optionally, enter a function by typing the function name and arguments directly from the keyboard, or by clicking on the **Function Wizard** button.

5. Repeat any combination of steps 2, 3, and 4 to complete the formula, then press ↵.

 **techno note**

To insert a cell reference into the active formula bar, you can click the cell with the mouse or select the cell by using the arrow keys. To insert a range reference, drag the mouse over the range or select the range by holding down **Shift** and pressing any combination of arrow keys. The word Point appears on the status bar and Excel displays a moving border around the range you have pointed to.

To step through the possible reference types—relative, absolute, and mixed—press **F4** repeatedly while the insertion point is positioned next to a reference in the formula bar. (See Copying Formulas on page 28 and References on page 96 for more information.)

To replace a formula with its current value while the formula bar is active, press **F9**.

You can enter formulas into each cell of a selected range in a single entry operation (See Copying Formulas on page 28 and References on page 96 for more information.)

Functions

A function is a tool that performs a predefined calculation or operation in Excel. Each function has a name and may require one or more arguments. (An argument supplies a specific item of information that the function requires to complete its defined calculation.) Excel has many built-in functions for specific categories of applications—for example, statistics, engineering, date and time operations, and so on.

new in Excel 5

Excel 5 provides a Function Wizard to help you enter functions and their arguments correctly into a worksheet.

To Enter a Function into a Worksheet Cell

1. Select the cell where you want to enter the function, and click the **Function Wizard** button on the Standard toolbar (or choose **Insert ➢ Function**). The resulting dialog box—Step 1 of the Function Wizard—has a list of function categories and a box that lists all the functions in a selected category.

2. Select a function category. Then, from the **Function Name** box, select the function that you want to enter into the active cell. (Use the vertical scroll bar to move up or down the **Function Name** box, or activate the box and type the first letter of the function you are looking for.) At the bottom of the Function Wizard dialog box you can read a brief description of the function you have selected.

3. Click **Next** to move to the next step of the Function Wizard.

4. The dialog box for Step 2 contains text boxes for each of the arguments required by the function you've selected. As you select each argument text box, the Function Wizard supplies a brief description of the information required in the argument. Type a value or an expression for each required argument; the value is displayed just to the right of the text box.

5. When you complete all the required arguments, the resulting value of the function is displayed at the upper-right corner of the Step 2 dialog box. Click **Finish** to enter the function and arguments into the current cell.

 shortcut

To display Step 1 of the Function Wizard dialog box, press **Shift-F3**.

Alternatively, select a cell, type =, and then type the name of the function you want to use. Press **Ctrl-A** and Excel opens Step 2 of the Function Wizard.

 **techno note**

You can express the arguments of a function in any form that meets the requirements of your worksheet. For example, an argument can appear as a value, a reference, a name, an ex-pression, another function, or some combination of these elements.

Headers and Footers

In a header or footer, you enter information that you want to repeat on each page of a printed worksheet. A header appears at the top of each page and a footer appears at the bottom. You can use headers and footers for information such as the date, the title of the document, and the page number.

To Create a Header or a Footer

1. Activate the worksheet on which you want to create a header or footer, and choose **File ➤ Page Setup**. Click the **Header/Footer** tab on the resulting dialog box.

2. The Header and Footer lists provide a selection of built-in header and footer suggestions, combining information such as the sheet name, the workbook name, the page number, the date, the registered user and company, and the title from the Summary Info window. To select one of these suggestions, click the arrow next to the **Header** or **Footer** box and click the text that you want to use. The corresponding sample box shows what the header or footer will look like. Notice that the built-in entries are divided by commas—for the left, center, and right sections of the header or footer.

3. To create a custom header or footer, click the **Custom Header** or **Custom Footer** button. The resulting dialog box divides the header or footer into three side-by-side sections labeled **Left Section**, **Center Section**, and **Right Section**.

4. Enter text into any or all of the three text boxes.

5. To include special information in a text box, type one of the following codes: **&[Page]** for the page number; **&[Pages]** for the number of pages; **&[Date]** for the date; **&[Time]** for the time; **&[File]** for the file name; **&[Tab]** for the sheet name.

6. Click **OK** to record your entries for the header or footer, and then click **OK** on the **Page Setup** dialog box.

By default, Excel provides a header that shows the file name at the top of each printed page, and a footer that displays the page number at the bottom of each page.

Figure 4 shows an example of a custom header definition. The left section of this header displays the current date (that is, the date when the worksheet is printed), the center section contains a worksheet title in boldface, and the right section shows the page number and the total number of pages. Here is how this header might appear at the top of a page of the worksheet:

7/12/93   Budget Worksheet   Page 3 of 5

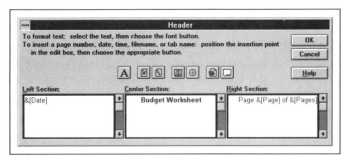

FIGURE 4: *A header definition*

 **shortcut**

To enter special codes into a section of the header or footer, you can click the **Page Number** button, the **Total Pages** button, the **Date** button, the **Time** button, or the **File Name** button. As shown in Figure 4, these buttons appear in a row just above the **Center Section** text box.

 tip

You can change the font or style of any text in a custom header or footer. For example, you might want to change a selection of text to boldface or italics, or increase its size. To do so, select the text and then click the **Font** button (labeled

A) in the **Header or Footer** dialog box. When the **Font** dialog box appears on the screen, select any combination of font, style, and size options, and click OK.

Help

The Excel Help window provides complete, practical information about Excel. There are several ways to open the Help window and locate the topics you need.

To Get Help

Try any of the following techniques:

⊙ Select **Help** ➢ **Contents**. Then select any one of the major topics in the **Contents** list. To go to an underlined topic in the Help window, click the topic with the mouse. (When you do so, the mouse pointer takes the shape of a pointing hand.)

⊙ Choose the **Search** command from the Help menu, and type a topic into the **Search** text box. Click the **Show Topics** button, and Excel displays a list of topics related to your entry. Select a topic and click the **Go To** button.

⊙ Click the **Help** button on the Standard toolbar. The mouse pointer turns into an arrow with a bold question mark. Click any object displayed in the Excel window to go directly to a relevant help topic. For example, click a button, a menu command, or a part of a window. The Help window then displays information about the object you have clicked.

⊙ Click the **Help** button on any dialog box to view instructions for carrying out the current command.

⊙ Press **F1** at any point in your work.

Hiding

Use the **Window** ➢ **Hide** command when you want to keep a workbook open but out of view. Within a worksheet, you can hide individual rows or columns when you want to keep specific ranges of data out of view.

To Hide an Open Workbook

Activate the workbook that you want to hide and choose **Window** ➢ **Hide**.

To Unhide a Workbook

Select **Window** ➢ **Unhide** (or **File** ➢ **Unhide** if no workbooks are displayed), select the name of the workbook you want to unhide, and click **OK**.

To Hide Columns or Rows on a Worksheet

1. Select the columns or rows that you want to hide.
2. Choose **Format** ➢ **Column** or **Format** ➢ **Row**.
3. In the resulting submenu, click **Hide**.

 shortcut

To hide a single column, drag the right border to the left border in the column heading. To hide a single row, drag the bottom border up to the top border in the row heading.

To Unhide Columns or Rows

1. Select the columns on both sides of the hidden columns or select the rows above and below the hidden rows.

2. Choose **Format ➢ Column** or **Format ➢ Row**.

3. On the resulting submenu, click **Unhide**.

 shortcut

To unhide a column, drag the thick border (representing the hidden column heading) to the right. While you drag, the mouse pointer appears as two parallel vertical lines with attached arrows. To unhide a row, drag the thick border (representing the hidden row heading) down. While you drag, the mouse pointer appears as two parallel horizontal lines with attached arrows.

Inserting

You can use either the **Insert** command or a special dragging technique to insert blank rows, blank columns, or a range of blank cells into a worksheet. When you do so, Excel shifts other cells down or to the right to make room for the insertion.

To Insert Entire Rows or Columns

1. Select the rows or columns at the position where you want to perform the insert operation. (To select a single row or column, click the row or column heading. To select more than one row or column, drag the mouse along the appropriate row or column headings.)

2. Choose **Insert ➢ Columns** or **Insert ➢ Rows**.

shortcut

Instead of choosing **Insert ➢ Columns** or **Insert ➢ Rows**, you can use a keyboard shortcut: Select the rows or columns and press **Ctrl+Shift+plus sign**.

To Insert a Range of Cells

1. Select the rectangular range at the position where you want to insert the blank cells.

2. Choose **Insert ➢ Cells**. The **Insert** dialog box appears.

3. Select **Shift Cells Right** or **Shift Cells Down**, depending on how you want Excel to make room for the new blank cells.

4. Click **OK**.

To Insert Cells by Dragging the Fill Handle

1. Select the cell or cells located *before* the position where you want to insert blank cells.

2. Hold down **Shift** and drag the fill handle down (to insert cells in rows) or to the right (to insert cells in columns). The amount of the insertion depends on how far you drag the fill handle.

To Insert Data Using Drag-and-Drop

1. Select the range of data that you want to copy and insert.

2. Position the mouse pointer along the border of the selection. The pointer shape changes to a white arrow.

3. Hold down **Ctrl** and **Shift** together. Then drag the mouse pointer to the location where you want to insert the copy range. A horizontal or vertical insertion bar follows the mouse pointer as you drag. To switch between a horizontal and vertical insertion, drag the mouse toward a column or row gridline in the target worksheet range.

4. Release the mouse button, then release the **Ctrl** and **Shift** keys. Excel copies the data from the copy range to the paste range and shifts existing entries down or to the right.

Links and 3-D References

A link between two worksheets is a means of sharing data and updating it when changes occur. Several kinds of links are possible in Excel 5:

- You can create a link between worksheets stored in different workbooks. In this case, the link is created by an *external reference* that identifies the source workbook and the location of the information within the workbook. The workbook that contains the external reference is known as a *dependent workbook*.

- You can also link worksheets that are stored within the same workbook. In this case, a reference identifies the source worksheet and the range of data.

- You can use 3-D *references* to combine data from multiple adjacent worksheets within a workbook. This kind of link is a convenient way to summarize large amounts of data stored in related worksheets.

To create a link, you can enter a reference directly from the keyboard or you can use the mouse to point to the source location. Or, if you want to let Excel create the link formula for you, simply click the **Paste Link** button in the **Edit ➤ Paste Special** dialog box.

To Create a Link between Two Workbooks

1. Open the workbooks that are to become the source and the destination in the link and activate the relevant worksheets on both workbooks. To view both workbooks at the same time, choose **Window ➤ Arrange**, select the **Tiled** option, and click **OK**.

2. On the source worksheet, select the data that will become the object of the link, and choose **Edit ➤ Copy**.

3. Activate the destination worksheet and select the cell where you want to establish the link.

4. Choose **Edit ➤ Paste Special**. In the **Paste Special** dialog box, click the **Paste Link** button. Excel enters an external reference into the destination worksheet.

 techno note

If both the source worksheet and the destination worksheet are open, the external reference appears in the following form:

```
=[workbook]worksheet!source
```

where *workbook* is the name of the source workbook, *worksheet* is the name of the source sheet, and *source* is the location of the data in the worksheet. Notice the punctuation: The workbook name is enclosed in square brackets, and the worksheet name and source location are separated by an exclamation point. (If the worksheet name contains one or more spaces, the workbook

68

name and worksheet name are enclosed in single quotation marks.) When you save the source worksheet to disk and then close it, Excel expands the external reference in the dependent workbook to include the directory path of the source workbook. In this case, the workbook name, its path, and the worksheet name are all enclosed in single quotation marks:

```
='path\[workbook]worksheet'!source
```

For example, an external reference might appear as:

```
'C:\EXCEL\[EXPENSES.XLS]NewProj'!$F$7
```

The exclamation point appears after the second single-quote character.

You can establish a link by entering an external formula directly into the dependent worksheet. The end result is the same as that of the Paste Link button. You can also create a link by entering a more complex external reference formula—that is, a formula that contains an external reference as one of several operands.

If the source data is in a range consisting of more than one cell, the **Paste Link** button enters the external formula as an array:

```
{=[workbook]worksheet!source}
```

To achieve the same effect directly from the keyboard, you can press Ctrl-Shift-↵ to enter an external array formula into the dependent worksheet.

The **Paste Link** button creates an absolute reference to the source range of data. Excel also permits external references consisting of relative or mixed references. When you copy such a formula within the dependent workbook, the relative reference is adjusted in the usual way, according to the position of the copy in relation to the original formula. (See *Copying Formulas* on page 28.)

If you open a dependent workbook at a time when the source workbook or workbooks are not open, Excel displays a dialog box asking you if you want to "reestablish links." Click **Yes**, and Excel checks the sources for any changes in data, and updates the destination accordingly.

To Create a Link between Worksheets on the Same Workbook

Select the source data on one worksheet, and choose **Edit ➢ Copy.** Then activate the destination worksheet, choose **Edit ➢ Paste Special**, and click the **Paste Link** button.

 **techno note**

In this case, the reference in the dependent worksheet has a simpler form:

```
=worksheet!source
```

where *worksheet* is the name of the source worksheet and *source* is the location of the data. If the worksheet name contains one or more spaces, it is enclosed in single quotation marks.

Another simple way to share data between worksheets in a workbook is to create book-level names for data in each source worksheet, and to use those names as references in the destination workbook. (See *Names* on page 76 for information about book-level versus sheet-level names.)

When you create a chart from a range of worksheet data in the same workbook, Excel enters SERIES formulas into the chart sheet. The arguments of the SERIES function are references to the source worksheet data, in the form *worksheet!source*. (See *Charting* on page 10 for more information.)

Creating a 3-D Formula

1. Within a workbook, develop two or more adjacent worksheets that contain related data. These worksheets will be the source of the data in the 3-D formula; they must be organized identically, with data entered into the same range on each sheet.

2. Activate the worksheet where you want to summarize the data in the source worksheets. Select the cell where you'll enter the 3-D formula.

3. Type an equal sign (=) and any other elements you want to include at the beginning of the formula. For example, enter the name of a function such as SUM, AVERAGE, MIN, or MAX; then enter the opening parenthesis for the function. (In this case, the 3-D reference will become the argument of the function.)

4. Click the tab of the first source worksheet. Then hold down Shift and click the tab of the last worksheet in the group. In the formula bar, Excel enters a sheet range such as 'Sheet2:Sheet4'. The range is followed by an exclamation point (!).

5. On the first source worksheet, click the cell or range that contains the data you want the 3-D formula to operate on. After the exclamation point in the fomula bar, Excel enters a reference to the cell or range you've selected.

6. Complete the formula (for example, by entering the closing parenthesis to complete a function) and press ↵ to enter the formula into the cell of the destination worksheet. Your 3-D formula is complete.

Lists

A list is a table of data stored in a worksheet. The top row of a list contains labels identifying the contents of each column. Subsequent rows contain records of information, all arranged in the same way. In previous versions of Excel, lists were known as *databases*; this term is still a valid alternative for describing a table of data.

Whether you think of a table as a list or a database, Excel 5 provides a variety of convenient and powerful operations that you can perform on the data:

- You can open a special *data form* dialog box that is designed to simplify several basic database operations, such as examining the data one record at a time, searching for records that match criteria, deleting records from the list, and adding new records to the list. (See *Data Form* on page 30 for more information.)

- You can use a *filter* to isolate rows of data that match specific criteria. With Excel's AutoFilter feature, you can apply a filter and view its result by making selections from drop-down lists of criteria. Alternatively, you can create a range of more complex criteria expressions and then choose the **Advanced Filter** command from the **Data ➤ Filter** submenu to find the matching records of information. (See *Filters* on page 46 and *Database Criteria* on page 37.)

- You can quickly rearrange the rows in a list—sorting the information alphabetically, numerically, or chronologically—by clicking one of the two **Sort** buttons on the Standard toolbar or by choosing **Data ➤ Sort**. (See *Sorting* on page 112 for details.)

- You can employ a special set of worksheet tools known as *database functions* to calculate statistical values on records that match certain criteria. For example, the DSUM function finds the sum of values in a particular field for selected records.

 tip

To perform these operations, begin by activating a worksheet that contains an appropriately formatted list, and in some cases selecting a cell inside the list. Unlike previous versions of the application, Excel 5 does not require additional steps for defining the range of a list or database.

Lotus 1-2-3 Help

Excel has an elaborate feature called Help for Lotus 1-2-3 Users that is designed to ease the transition between 1-2-3 and Excel. This feature provides either instructions for accomplishing 1-2-3 tasks in Excel, or actual demonstrations of the tasks.

To Use the Help for Lotus 1-2-3 Users Feature

1. Select **Help** ➢ **Lotus 1-2-3**. The Help for Lotus 1-2-3 Users dialog box appears on the screen.

2. In the Help Options group, select **Instructions** if you want to see a list of steps for a task, or **Demo** if you want Excel to demonstrate a task. (If you select **Demo**, you may also adjust the pace of the demonstration by clicking the **Faster** or **Slower** button.)

3. Choose a sequence of 1-2-3 commands from the **Menu** box. To go through a command sequence, you can double-click the command names in the list, or you can

type letters at the keyboard just as you would do in
Lotus 1-2-3.

4. As you go through the command sequence, the Help
dialog box shows you the steps for accomplishing the
same procedure in Excel.

5. When you reach the end of the sequence, press ↵ or
click **OK**. If you have requested instructions, Excel displays a text box with numbered steps. You can keep
this box on the screen while you perform the steps of
the procedure. If you have requested a demo, Excel
elicits any required information from you and then
begins the demonstration.

 shortcut

Choose **Tools** ➤ **Options** and click the **Transition** tab. Select
the **Lotus 1-2-3 Help** option, and then click **OK**. Under this
setting you can simply press the slash key (/) to open the
Help for Lotus 1-2-3 Users dialog box at any time during
your work.

Moving Data

You can move data from one range of worksheet cells to another by using the familiar **Cut** and **Paste** commands, or by
dragging the range with the mouse.

To Move Data Using Cut and Paste

1. Select the range of data you want to move.

2. Choose **Edit** ➤ **Cut**.

3. Select the upper-left corner of the location to which you want to move the data.

4. Choose **Edit ➤ Paste**.

 shortcut

Ctrl+X is the keyboard shortcut for Cut, and **Ctrl+V** is the shortcut for Paste.

 warning

Proceed cautiously when you move formulas that contain references. If you move a formula alone—without moving the range of data that it refers to—the references remain fixed, and the result of the formula does not change. If you move a formula along with the entire range it refers to, Excel adjusts the references accordingly, but again the result of the formula remains the same. However, you should generally avoid moving a formula along with only part of the range of data it refers to.

To Move a Range by Dragging

1. Select the range that you want to move.

2. Position the mouse pointer along the border of the selection. The pointer becomes a white arrow.

3. Drag the selection to its new position in the worksheet. While you drag, an empty frame represents the selection that you are moving.

4. Release the mouse button. The entire selection moves to its new location.

reminder

To insert the selection between existing blocks of data, hold down **Shift** while you drag. A horizontal or vertical line represents the position to which the data will be moved and inserted. Release the mouse button to complete the move. See *Inserting* on page 65 for more information.

Names

A name is an identifier that you define to represent a cell or range on a worksheet or macro sheet. You can use commands from the **Insert** ➤ **Name** submenu to assign names to cells and ranges, or you can enter a new name directly into the name box on the formula bar.

Once you have defined one or more names, you can use them to clarify the meaning of formulas you write: a name takes the place of a cell or range reference, resulting in formulas that people can understand more readily. You can also define names to represent values or formulas that are not actually entered into worksheet cells.

Names in Excel 5 can have book-level or sheet-level *scope*. A book-level name is available anywhere within a workbook, and is therefore a convenient way to create references between worksheets. A sheet-level name is explicitly available only in the worksheet where it is defined, and is a means of avoiding ambiguity when you want to use the same name for ranges in several different worksheets.

To Define a Name

1. Select the cell or range to which you want to assign a name. Choose **Insert ➢ Name**. Then choose the **Define** command in the **Name** submenu. The **Define Name** dialog box appears on the screen.

2. Enter a name into the **Names in Workbook** box, and click **OK**.

 shortcut

Press Ctrl-F3 to display the **Define Name** dialog box.

 **techno note**

A name must begin with a letter or an underscore character, and may contain letters, digits, backslashes, underscores, question marks, and periods. Spaces are not allowed. Instead of a space you can use an underscore character or capitalization to clarify the meaning of a name; for example:

    Base_Usage

    BaseUsage

Although you might choose to make use of capitalization in this way, alphabetic case in names is not significant to Excel. For example, Excel considers the names *BaseUsage*, *BASEUSAGE*, and *baseusage* to be the same. A name can be as long as 255 characters, although names are typically short enough to be entered easily into a formula.

If you select a cell or range that contains a text entry—or is located below or to the right of a cell that contains a text entry—the **Define Name** dialog box suggests the text for the name.

In the **Refers to** box of the **Define Name** dialog box, you can enter any cell or range reference, beginning with an equal sign, =. (The default entry is a reference to the selected cell or range.) In practice, names usually represent absolute references, though Excel allows you to define a name for a relative or mixed reference. You can also enter a numeric or text value or an entire formula into the **Refers to** box; in this case, the name you define represents a value or formula that is not present on the worksheet itself.

The **Names in Workbook** box contains a list of all the names that are already defined for the current workbook sheet. You can delete a name's definition by highlighting the name in the list and clicking the **Delete** button. When you do so, any formula that uses the deleted name results in a #NAME? error value.

To Create a Name in the Name Box

1. Select the cell or range to which you want to assign a name.

2. Click the name box, located at the left side of the formula bar.

3. Enter a name for the selected range and press ↵.

To Create Names from Text Entries

1. Select a range that includes text entries that you want to assign as names to corresponding cells, rows, or columns in the range selection. The text entries can appear on the top or bottom row and/or the left or right column of the selection.

2. Choose **Insert** ➢ **Name**. Then choose **Create** from the **Name** submenu.

3. In the **Create Names** dialog box, select any combination of the four check box options: **Top Row**, **Left Column**, **Bottom Row**, and **Right Column**. Then click **OK**. Excel assigns names from the indicated rows and columns to the corresponding adjacent cells in the range.

 shortcut

Press **Ctrl-Shift-F3** to display the **Create Names** dialog box.

To Go to a Named Cell or Range

Choose **Edit** ➤ **Goto**, select a name from the list of defined names, and click **OK**.

 shortcut

Press F5 to display the **Goto** dialog box. Alternatively, click the down-arrow button located just to the right of the name box on the formula bar. In the resulting drop-down list, click the name of the cell or range that you want to select.

To Paste a Name into a Formula

Choose **Insert** ➤ **Name**, and then choose **Paste** from the **Name** submenu. In the **Paste Name** dialog box, select a name from the list of defined names, and click OK. Excel activates the formula bar (if you have not already begun a formula) and enters the name as an operand in the formula.

shortcut

Press **F3** to view the **Paste Name** dialog box—either while
you are entering a formula into the formula bar, or before you
begin the formula.

To Apply Names to an Existing Formula

1. Select a cell or range containing one or more formulas.
   The references in the formulas should be ones for
   which you have defined names.

2. Choose **Insert ➤ Names**. Then choose **Apply** from the
   Names submenu. In the **Apply Names** list, select all the
   names that you want to apply to the current formula.

3. Click **OK**. Excel replaces references with names in the
   currently selected formulas.

Number Formats

The **Number** tab in the **Format Cells** dialog box provides a
variety of predefined formats that you can use to change the
appearance of numeric entries in a worksheet. The format
categories include **Number**, **Accounting**, **Text**, **Currency**,
Date, **Time**, **Percentage**, **Fraction**, and **Scientific**.

To Format Numeric Values in a Worksheet

1. Select the cell or range of values that you want to format.

2. Choose **Format ➤ Cells**. Click the **Number** tab in the
   resulting dialog box.

3. Select the name of a format category. In response, Excel lists the codes for all the predefined formats that are available in the category you have selected.

4. Select a format code and click OK.

Figure 5 shows examples of formatted entries in the major format categories.

	A	B	C	D	E	F	G
	Number	Currency	Date	Time	Percent	Fraction	Scientific
1	Number	Currency	Date	Time	Percent	Fraction	Scientific
2	22,128.89	$34,699.66	11/20/17	6:00 AM	51.13%	1089 35/58	4.55E+06
3	24,283.29	$7,367.55	5/13/21	4:13 AM	46.23%	873 3/56	2.76E+04
4	45,392.60	$21,872.89	2/14/95	6:07 AM	24.93%	502 5/36	6.02E+06
5	(6,636.18)	($5,082.89)	6/2/93	1:24 AM	98.52%	8 31/86	5.49E+02
6	88,610.24	$62,279.00	12/1/72	4:24 AM	34.53%	404 70/73	6.85E-06
7	58,235.11	$48,140.87	8/16/34	10:14 AM	57.16%	47295 7/13	4.16E+06
8	10,621.98	$39,595.55	7/1/61	4:14 PM	90.96%	8650 1/16	9.29E+02
9	(3,397.57)	$68,668.40	10/31/36	7:37 PM	74.30%	6 61/95	1.20E+06
10	7,984.37	$35,666.61	11/28/07	10:31 PM	77.71%	156 7/9	4.99E+06
11	20,839.03	($1,245.58)	11/21/92	6:35 PM	43.12%	23/88	6.35E-04

FORMATS.XLS

Sheet1 / Sheet2 / Sheet3 / Sheet4 / Sheet5 / Sheet6 / Sheet7 / She

FIGURE 5: *Examples of number formats*

recommended

When you enter a date or time value in a cell, type the entry in one of Excel's predefined date or time formats. Excel recognizes the value as a chronological entry and automatically applies the appropriate format to the cell. (The numeric value actually stored in the cell is a *serial date* or *serial time* value. See *Date and Time Entries* on page 39 for details.)

Opening Files

Use **File** ➤ **Open** to open workbooks from disk. Use **File** ➤ **New** to create new Excel workbooks.

To Open an Excel Document from Disk

1. Select **File** ➤ **Open**.

2. If necessary, use the **Directories** and **Drives** list boxes to find the path that contains the file you want to open. (Double-click an entry in the **Directories** list to open a selected directory.)

3. Select the document's name from the **File Name** list, and click **OK**.

 shortcut

To display the **Open** dialog box, you can click the the **Open** button in the Standard toolbar.

 recommended

If the file you want to open is among the four most recently opened files, select the file from the list of names at the bottom of the **File** menu.

 tip

If you want to examine a document but not change its contents, click the **Read Only** option on the **Open** dialog box. If you make changes in the file, Excel will allow you to save the file under a new name, but not update the file under its existing name.

To Open a New Excel Workbook

Select **File ➢ New**.

 shortcut

To open a new workbook, you can click the **New Workbook** button in the Standard toolbar.

Page Setup

⊚ ⊚ ⊚ ⊚ ⊚ ⊚ ⊚ ⊚ ⊚ ⊚ ⊚ ⊚ ⊚ ⊚ ⊚ ⊚ ⊚ ⊚ ⊚ ⊚

The **File ➢ Page Setup** command gives you control over the layout of sheets that you print from a workbook.

To Select Options for Printing a Worksheet

Activate a worksheet, choose **File ➢ Page Setup**, and select options from any of the tabs that appear on the **Page Setup** dialog box:

⊚ Click the **Page** tab. Select **Portrait** to print the document from the top to the bottom of the paper, or **Landscape** to print the document sideways. In the **Scaling** box, enter a value less than 100% to reduce the size of a printed document, or a value greater than 100% to enlarge the printed document. Alternatively, click the **Fit To** option button if you want Excel to scale the document automatically to fit the number of pages you specify. Select an option from the **Paper Size** list. The sizes include standard paper dimensions such as letter, legal, and executive, along with standard envelope sizes. Select a **Print Quality** option of **High**, **Medium**, **Low**, or **Draft**. Finally, if you want the page numbering to start at some point other than 1, enter a value in the **First Page Number** box. (By default, page numbers are printed in the footer. See *Headers and Footers* on page 60 for details.)

◉ Click the **Margins** tab. Enter measurements for the top, bottom, left, and right margins, and for the position of the header and footer. To center the document on the page, click one or both of the **Center on Page** check boxes, labeled **Horizontally** and **Vertically**.

◉ Click the **Header/Footer** tab, and enter information about the header and footer you want printed on each page. (See *Headers and Footers* on page 60 for details.)

◉ Click the **Sheet** tab. Optionally, enter a reference in the Print Area box. (Alternatively, you can select a **Print What** option in the **Print** dialog box. See *Printing Worksheets* on page 93 for details.) If you want to print certain rows or columns of information as "titles" on each page, select the **Rows to Repeat at Top** and/or **Columns to Repeat at Left** box and point to the rows or columns that contain the titles. Select any combination of options in the **Print** group: keep the X in the **Cell Gridlines** check box if you want to print the gridlines; select the **Notes** option if you want the printout to include notes you have stored in worksheet cells; select **Draft Quality** for faster printing; select the **Black and White** check box for black and white printing; and select the **Row and Column Headings** check box if you want to print the sheet's row numbers and column letters.

In the **Page Order** box, select one of the two options—
Down, then Across; or **Across, then Down**—to specify
how to organize pagination in a multipage document.

 **techno note**

If the active sheet is a chart, the **Sheet** tab is replaced by the
Chart tab on the **Page Setup** dialog box. Select one of the
three options in the **Printed Chart Size** box: Use **Full Page**,
Scale to Fit Page, or **Custom**. You can also select **Printing
Quality** options. (See *Printing Charts* on page 91 for details.)

A column of command buttons appears on the right side of
the **Page Setup** dialog box. Click the **Print** button to open the
Print dialog box and print the document. Click **Print Preview**
to preview your document before printing it. Click **Options** to
open the Setup dialog box for your printer.

Panes

By dividing a worksheet into panes, you can view two or four
different parts of the sheet at once.

To Divide a Sheet into Panes

1. Select the row, column, or cell at which you want to
divide the sheet.

2. Choose **Window ➢ Split**.

The **Split** command creates two or four panes, depending on
the range or cell selection at the time you choose the command:

◉ To create two panes that are split vertically, select an
entire column or a single cell in row 1 (other than cell A1).

⊙ To create two panes split horizontally, select an entire row or a single cell in column A (other than cell A1).

⊙ To create four panes, select any cell except in row 1 or column A.

⊙ To create four panes of approximately equal size, select cell A1.

Figure 6 shows an empty worksheet split into four panes.

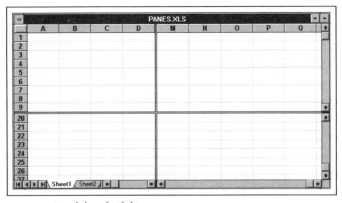

FIGURE 6: *A worksheet divided into panes*

 recommended

You can create panes visually by dragging one or both of the *split bars*. The split bars are small black rectangles, initially located at the right end of the horizontal scroll bar and at the top of the vertical scroll bar. To divide a worksheet into two vertical panes, drag the vertical split bar to the right across the horizontal scroll bar. To create two horizontal panes, drag the horizontal split bar down the vertical scroll bar. Alternatively, double-click a split bar to create two panes that are approximately the same size.

 **techno note**

Scrolling actions are synchronized in the panes of a split sheet: With a horizontal split, the same columns are displayed in both panes during horizontal scrolling; and with a vertical split, the same rows are displayed during vertical scrolling.

To Freeze the Panes

Choose **Window** ➢ **Freeze Panes** to prevent the top pane from scrolling vertically, or the left pane from scrolling horizontally. This may be useful if the left or top pane contains labels or other data that you want to keep in view, even while you scroll in the other panes.

 tip

Choose **Window** ➢ **Unfreeze Panes** to restore the original scrolling capabilities of a split worksheet.

To Remove Panes from a Sheet

Select **Window** ➢ **Remove Split**.

shortcut

Alternatively, double-click a split bar to send it back to its initial position.

Patterns

ⓔ ⓔ ⓔ ⓔ ⓔ ⓔ ⓔ ⓔ ⓔ ⓔ ⓔ ⓔ ⓔ ⓔ ⓔ ⓔ ⓔ ⓔ ⓔ ⓔ

You can use options on the **Patterns** tab of the **Format** Cells dialog box to apply shading to a range of cells on a worksheet.

To Apply Shading to a Range of Cells

1. Select the range, choose **Format ➤ Cells**, and click the **Patterns** tab. The resulting dialog box contains a **Color** palette, a **Pattern** box, and a **Sample** box.

2. Click the drop-down arrow at the right side of the **Pattern** box, and select a shading pattern from the top three rows of the resulting palette. Optionally, click the drop-down arrow a second time, and select a color for the pattern.

3. In the **Color** palette, select a color for the background of the pattern.

4. Examine the result of your selections in the Sample box. If the pattern appears the way you want it, click **OK**.

shortcut

Point to the selected range, click the right mouse button, and choose **Format Cells** from the shortcut menu.

Previewing

The **File** ➤ **Print Preview** command displays a preview window in which you can see how a worksheet will look on the printed page. This window gives you the opportunity to examine the document's layout, formatting, and contents before you actually print it.

To Preview a Document Before You Print It

Activate the document that you want to preview, choose **File** ➤ **Print Preview**. As you can see in Figure 7, the preview window displays a full-page picture of the active document. Across the top of the window you see a variety of tools you can use to study or modify the document to be printed:

⊚ Click the **Next** or **Previous** tool to scroll to the next or previous page in the document. (These buttons are dimmed if the document consists of only one page.)

⊚ Click the **Zoom** button to enlarge the view of the printed document. (Alternatively, point to the document itself and click the mouse button when you see the magnifying glass pointer.) In the **Zoom** mode, use the scroll bars to move up, down, or across the document. To return to the regular page preview display, click the mouse anywhere on the zoomed document.

⊚ Click the **Print** button to open the **Print** dialog box, or the **Setup** button to open the **Page Setup** dialog box.

⊚ Click the **Margin** button if you want to adjust margins in your document. Excel displays margin lines and handles that you can drag to make visual adjustments in the top, bottom, left, or right margins. Click the **Margin** button again to remove the margin handles from the window.

● Click **Close** to return to your document in the Excel application window.

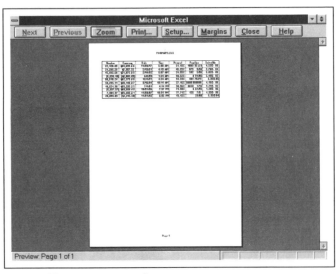

FIGURE 7: *The Print Preview window*

 **shortcut**

Click the **Print Preview** button on the **Standard** toolbar.

Printer Setup

To select a printer on a system that includes more than one, you can click the **Printer Setup** button on the **Print** dialog box (**File ➤ Print**). To change a printer's operational settings, you

90

then click the **Setup** button on the **Printer Setup** dialog box. Printer settings for a given driver are used by all the applications you run in Windows.

To Change the Printer Settings

1. Choose **File** ➤ **Print** and then click the **Printer Setup** button on the **Print** dialog box.

2. Select a printer driver from the list. If you have no changes to make in the settings of this driver, click **OK** to return to the **Print** dialog box.

3. If you want to change the settings of the driver you've selected, click the **Setup** button on the **Printer Setup** dialog box. The options displayed in the resulting **Setup** dialog box vary according to the characteristics and capabilities of a given printer.

4. After you change the printer settings, click **OK** on the **Setup** and **Printer Setup** dialog boxes. This returns you to the Print dialog box.

 shortcut

You can also get to the **Setup** dialog box by choosing **File** ➤ **Page Setup** and then clicking the **Options** button.

Printing Charts

To print a chart, begin by double-clicking an embedded chart object or clicking the tab of a chart sheet. Using the **File** ➤ **Page Setup** command, you can then specify how you want the chart to appear on the printed page.

To Print a Chart

1. Activate the chart that you want to print.

2. Select **File** ➤ **Page Setup**. In the **Page Setup** dialog box, click the **Chart** tab, and then select one of the three option buttons in the **Printed Chart Size** group:

  - ◉ **Use Full Page** stretches the chart over the length and width of the page.

  - ◉ **Scale to Fit Page** fills as much of the printed page as possible, while maintaining the height-to-width ratio that you have established in the chart.

  - ◉ **Custom** prints the chart in the same size as the chart you have produced.

3. Click **OK**. Then choose **File** ➤ **Print** to open the **Print** dialog box. Enter a new value in the Copies text box if you want to print more than one copy of the chart. Click **OK** to begin printing.

 shortcut

To bypass the **Print** dialog box and begin printing immediately, click the **Print** button on the Standard toolbar.

 tip

When you print a full-color screen chart on a black-and-white printer, Excel selects shades of gray along with black and white to substitute for the colors. The effect may be clearer and visually more effective if you select the **Print in Black and White** option in the **Chart** tab of the **Page Setup** dialog box. Experiment with this option and decide which you prefer.

Printing Worksheets

The **File** ➢ **Print** command gives you the options of printing a selection of worksheet data, the active sheet, a selection of sheets, or an entire workbook.

To Print Information from a Workbook

1. Open and activate the workbook that contains the information you want to print.

2. Make one of the following selections:

- Select a range if you want to print a selection of data.

- Activate a worksheet if you want to print that sheet alone.

- Select two or more sheets if you want to print multiple sheets in one operation. (To select a range of contiguous sheets, click the tab of the first sheet, hold down **Shift**, and then click the tab of the last sheet. To select noncontiguous sheets, hold down **Ctrl** while you click the tabs of the sheets you want to include in the selection. See *Workbooks* on page 120 for more information.)

- Activate any sheet if you want to print the entire workbook.

3. Choose **File** ➢ **Print**. The **Print** dialog box appears.

4. Select an option in the **Print What** group:

- Click the **Selection** option to print a range you have selected. (If you select this option, Excel ignores any **Print Area** specified in the **Page Setup** dialog box.)

- Click the **Selected Sheets** option to print the active sheet or the multiple sheets you have selected.

- Click **Entire Workbook** to print sheets or designated print areas on all the sheets of the workbook.

5. If you want to change any aspect of the page layout, click the **Page Setup** button and select options in the various tabs of the resulting dialog box. (See *Page Setup* on page 83 for details.) Click **OK** to return to the Print dialog box.

6. In the **Copies** box, enter the number of copies if you want more than one.

7. In the **Print Range** group, click **Pages** and enter a range of page numbers in the **From** and **To** boxes if you want to print less than the entire document.

8. Click **OK** to begin printing.

 shortcut

Click the **Print** tool on the Standard toolbar to print the document immediately without viewing the **Print** dialog box.

To Set a Manual Page Break

1. Activate the worksheet on which you want to define a page break.

2. Select a column for a vertical page break, a row for a horizontal page break, or a single cell for both.

3. Choose **Insert ➤ Page Break**.

 **techno note**

Manual page breaks appear just above a selected row, just to the left of a selected column, or just above and to the left of a selected cell. Excel marks manual page breaks with a line of dashes. If you do not set manual page breaks, Excel calculates automatic page breaks appropriate for the page size and the margin settings.

To remove a manual page break, select the row, column, or cell where the page break is located, and choose **Insert ➤ Remove Page Break.**

Recalculation

Whenever you change an entry on a worksheet, Excel normally recalculates all formulas that are affected by the new entry. In other words, *recalculation* is automatic by default in Excel. But you may sometimes want to switch to *manual* recalculation—for example, when you are working on a detailed worksheet that contains complex formulas. Under the manual setting, Excel recalculates open worksheets only when you give the word.

To Switch to Manual Recalculation

1. Select **Tools ➤ Options**, and click the **Calculation** tab.

2. In the **Calculation** group, select the **Manual** option button, and then click **OK**.

tip

Under the manual recalculation setting, the status bar displays the word *Calculate* whenever a change takes place that would affect the result of a dependent formula. When you see the word *Calculate*, you know that one or more formulas need to be recalculated.

To Recalculate Manually

Press the **F9** function key.

 reminder

When you press **F9**, Excel recalculates the dependent formulas on all open worksheets. The word *Calculate* disappears from the status bar. To recalculate only the active worksheet, press **Shift+F9**.

 tip

Automatic recalculation is the normal mode of operation in Excel. To switch back to automatic recalculation, choose **Tools ➤ Options**, click the **Calculation** tab, click the **Automatic** option button, and click **OK**.

References

A *reference* identifies the position of a cell or a range of cells on a worksheet. In a formula, a reference stands for the value stored in a cell or the values stored in a range.

For the purposes of copying a formula from one cell to another in a worksheet, you can write a reference in any of three types, depending on how you want the reference to appear in copies of the formula:

- An *absolute* reference is copied unchanged from one cell to another.

- A *relative* reference is adjusted according to the position of the copy.

- A *mixed* reference is a combination of absolute and relative references.

An *external* reference identifies a cell or range on another workbook, and creates a link between two workbooks.

To Change a Reference Type in the Formula Bar

1. Position the insertion point just after the reference in the active formula bar. (For a range, highlight the entire reference.)

2. Press the **F4** function key repeatedly to step through the possible refrence types: from relative to absolute to mixed.

 reminder

Excel uses dollar signs to denote absolute or mixed references. For example, consider the following forms of the reference to cell E9:

- E9 is an absolute reference. When you copy a formula containing this E9 as an operand, the reference is copied unchanged and always refers to cell E9.

- E$9 is a mixed reference, where the column reference (E) is relative and the row reference ($9) is absolute. When you copy a formula containing E$9 as an operand, the reference to row 9 remains fixed, but the reference to column E can change relative to the column of the copied formula.

- $E9 is a mixed reference, where the the column reference ($E) is absolute and the row reference (9) is relative. When you copy a formula containing $E9 as an operand, the reference to column E remains fixed, but the reference to row 9 can change relative to the row of the copied formula.

- E9 is a relative reference, where both the column and the row are relative. When you copy a formula containing E9 as an operand, both the column and the row can change relative to the position of the copied formula.

See *Copying Formulas* on page 28 for more information.

 tip

By pressing **F4** four times, you can step through the complete cycle of reference types and back to the original reference.

 **techno note**

Excel has an alternate reference style, known as R1C1, in which both columns and rows are numbered on the worksheet. (Users who have worked with spreadsheet programs other than Excel may be more accustomed to the R1C1 reference style.) To switch between the A1 and R1C1 styles, choose **Tools ➢ Options**, click the **General** tab, and select an option in the **Reference Style** group.

To Create an External Reference

1. Open the workbooks that will become the source and the destination of the data and activate the target worksheets in both workbooks. For convenience, choose **Window ➢ Arrange**, select **Tiled**, and click **OK**, to display the two windows side-by-side on the screen.

2. Select the cell in the destination workbook where you want to create an external reference.

3. Enter an equal sign (**=**) to begin a formula.

4. Activate the source worksheet, point to the cell for which you want to create a reference, and click the mouse button. Excel creates an external reference on the destination workbook.

5. Press ⏎ to complete the formula.

 see also

Links and 3-D References (page 67)

Repeating Commands

The **Edit ➢ Repeat** command gives you a quick way to repeat the last operation you performed in Excel.

To Repeat the Previous Command

Choose **Edit ➢ Repeat**.

shortcut

The keyboard shortcut for **Edit ➤ Repeat** is **Alt+↵**. Or click the **Repeat** button on the **Standard** toolbar.

tip

You can perform a task on one workbook—such as a formatting command or a page setup operation—and then repeat the same task on another workbook. After completing your work on the first workbook, select the second workbook and then choose **Edit ➤ Repeat**.

warning

If the previous command cannot be repeated, **Repeat** is dimmed in the **Edit** menu, or the command is displayed as **Can't Repeat**.

Replacing Worksheet Data

The **Edit ➤ Replace** command searches for an entry in a worksheet and replaces it with another entry.

To Replace Data in a Worksheet

1. Activate the sheet in which you want to replace data; then choose **Edit ➤ Replace**. The **Replace** dialog box appears on the screen.

100

2. In the **Find What** box, enter the text that you want to replace.

3. In the **Replace With** box, enter the replacement text.

4. In the **Search** list, select **By Rows** to search from the top to the bottom of your worksheet, or **By Columns** to search from left to right.

5. Click the **Match Case** option, placing an X in its check box, if you want Excel to search for the text in the exact uppercase and lowercase combinations you entered into the **Find What** box. Leave this option unchecked if you want to perform the search without regard for alphabetic case.

6. Click the **Find Entire Cells Only** option, placing an X in its check box, if the text you have entered in the **Find What** box represents an entire cell entry; leave the option unchecked if you want to search for the text as a portion of a cell entry.

7. To carry out the search-and-replace operation, use any sequence of the following command buttons:

- Click **Find Next** to find the next occurrence of the **Find What** text, or hold down **Shift** and click **Find Next** to find the previous occurrence.

- Click **Replace** to replace the target text in the current cell and then find the next occurrence.

- Click **Replace All** to replace all the remaining occurrences of the target text and close the **Replace** dialog box.

- Click **Close** to close the **Replace** dialog box without changing any additional entries.

If Excel does not find the target text in your worksheet, a dialog box appears on the screen with the message *Cannot find matching data to replace*. If the search is unsuccessful, but you

believe the text does exist in your worksheet, reopen the
Replace dialog box and make sure you have selected the
appropriate option in the **Find What** box, and the correct
setting for the **Match Case** option.

warning

Be careful about using **Edit** ➢ **Replace** in a worksheet that
contains formulas. The search-and-replace operation works on
the formula entries themselves, not on the results of formulas.
If a replacement produces in an invalid formula—that is, a
formula that Excel can't work with—an error will result.

reminder

If **Edit** ➢ **Replace** produces unexpected results, immediately
choose **Edit** ➢ **Undo Replace** (or press **Ctrl+Z**).

tip

You can use wildcard characters in the search text: **?** stands for
a single unspecified character, and ***** stands for a string of unspecified characters.

recommended

To restrict the search-and-replace operation to a specific range
of cells on your worksheet, select the range before choosing

102

Edit ➢ Replace. Otherwise, Excel searches through the entire worksheet for the target text.

Row Height

Adjusting the height of a row allows you to display multiple lines of text within a single cell, or to display large or small font sizes within the row.

To Change the Height of a Single Row

1. Select a cell in the row, or click the row heading to select the entire row.

2. Choose **Format ➢ Row**. Choose **Height** on the resulting submenu.

3. Enter a new value in the **Row Height** text box and then click **OK**.

To change the heights of a group of rows, select the rows and then choose **Format ➢ Row** and choose **Height**.

recommended

Alternatively, you can use the mouse to adjust a row's height visually. To do so, position the mouse pointer over the line located just under the row's heading at the left side of the worksheet window, and drag the line down (to increase the height) or up (to decrease the height). Double-click the line to adjust the row height to the best fit for the current contents.

tip

In the example shown in Figure 8, cell A1 contains a three-line text entry that is displayed in a larger size than the rest of the worksheet. The height of row 1 has been increased accordingly.

	A	B	C
1	**XYZ Corp. Product Sales 1993**		
2		**Q1**	**Q2**
3	Product 1	9843	5805
4	Product 2	6762	7109
5	Product 3	4952	6655

FIGURE 8: *Adjusting row height for a multiline text entry*

To create a multiline title like this one, follow these general steps:

1. Select the cell, and type a line of text. Then press **Alt+↵** to insert a carriage return into the entry. The height of the formula bar increases to accommodate the next line of the entry. (The height of the active worksheet cell remains unchanged at this point in the procedure.)

2. Repeat step 1 for each line of text that you want to include in the entry.

3. Press ↵ to complete the entry. Excel automatically wraps the text in the cell, but not necessarily in the same line arrangement as your original entry.

4. If the column is too narrow to display the lines of text in the way you entered them, increase the column width and then adjust the row height to produce the effect you want.

104

 **techno note**

The *standard* row height row is the best fit for the largest font displayed in the row. Excel automatically adjusts the height of a row when you change the font of an entry in the row.

Saving Files

The **File** ➤ **Save As** and **File** ➤ **Save** commands are for saving workbooks to disk. Use **File** ➤ **Save As** to save a file for the first time. Use **File** ➤ **Save** to update a file after you have made changes in a workbook.

To Save a Workbook to Disk for the First Time

1. Choose **File** ➤ **Save As**.

2. If necessary, use the **Directories** and **Drives** list boxes to select a path for saving the file. (Double-click an entry in the **Directories** list to open a selected directory.)

3. Enter a name for the workbook in the **File Name** box. (Excel adds XLS as the default extension for the file name.)

4. Click **OK** to save the file.

 shortcut

F12 is the keyboard shortcut for opening the Save As dialog box. Alternatively, you can click the **Save** button on the **Standard** toolbar; if the active workbook has not been saved yet as a file on disk, Excel opens the **Save As** dialog box.

 **techno note**

You may sometimes want to save a file in a format that can be used with software other than Excel—for example, Lotus 1-2-3 or dBase. To do so, open the **Save As** dialog box, and click the arrow next to the box labeled **Save File as Type**. Select a format from the list that appears in the dialog box.

 tip

Click the **Options** button on the **Save As** dialog box for additional features related to the save operation. For example, you can create a password for restricting access to the current file. In addition, the **Save Options** dialog box has a check box labeled **Always Create Backup**. If you check this option, Excel automatically maintains a backup copy (with extension name BAK) each time you save the file.

To Update a File after Making Changes

Choose **File** ➤ **Save**.

 shortcut

Click the **Save** button on the **Standard** toolbar.

Selecting a Range

Excel provides a variety of convenient mouse and keyboard techniques for making selections on a worksheet. You can use

106

these techniques to select a single cell, a range of cells, or a group of noncontiguous ranges on a worksheet.

To Select a Cell

Click the cell with the mouse, or move the cell pointer by pressing any combination of arrow keys— →, ←, ↓, or ↑.

recommended

To move quickly to the beginning or end of a block of data in a worksheet, hold down **Ctrl** and press an arrow key in the direction you want to move. Alternatively, press the **End** key and then press an arrow key. (The notation END appears on the status bar when you press **End**.)

To Select a Range

Drag the mouse over the range, or hold down **Shift** and press any combination of arrow keys.

tip

Excel provides another keyboard technique for selecting a range: Press the **F8** function key to toggle into Extend mode, and then press any combination of arrow keys to select the range. The notation EXT appears on the status bar. Press **Esc** or **F8** again to toggle out of Extend mode.

To Select Noncontiguous Ranges

Select the first range, then hold down **Ctrl** while you select additional ranges with the mouse.

In the notation for noncontiguous ranges, each reference in the list is separated from the next by a comma.

To Select a Row or Column

Click the row heading or column heading with the mouse, or press **Shift+Spacebar** for a row or **Ctrl+Spacebar** for a column.

To Select an Entire Worksheet

Click the **Select All** button located at the intersection of the row and column headings (near the upper-left corner of the worksheet), or press **Ctrl+Shift+Spacebar**.

Series

The **Series** command in the **Edit** ➢ **Fill** submenu is a versatile tool for entering a *series* of numeric or date values in a work-sheet range. In this context, a series is a sequence of values in which the entries are calculated from a *linear* or *exponential* for-mula. In the **Series** dialog box, you choose the type of series you want to create, and you provide specific values that de-termine the content of the series:

- ◉ The *step value* is used to calculate each successive element of the series.

- ◉ The *stop value* determines the end of the series.

108

The *start value* is an existing entry in the worksheet range where you create the series.

To Create a Series

1. In the first cell of a row or column range on the active worksheet, enter the initial value for the series you want to create. Then select the range for the series.

2. Choose **Edit ➤ Fill** and choose the **Series** command from the submenu. The **Series** dialog box displays three groups of option buttons, labeled **Series in**, **Type**, and **Date Unit**. For the **Series in** option, Excel automatically selects **Rows** or **Columns** according to the range you have already selected on the worksheet.

3. In the **Type** group, select the type of data series you want to create. If you select **Date**, Excel activates the **Date Unit** group. Select one of the unit options in the this group.

4. Optionally, enter a value in the **Step Value** box. (The default is 1.)

5. Optionally, enter a value in the **Stop Value** box.

6. Click **OK** to create the series.

techno note

Excel's use of the **Step Value** entry depends on the type of series you select:

- For a linear series, the step value is *added* to each value to produce the next value in the series.

- For a growth series, each value is *multiplied* by the step value to produce the next value in the series. (Normally you'll supply a value other than 1 as the **Step Value** for a growth series.)

- For a date series, the step value represents the number of days between one entry and the next in the series. (You can further refine the steps of a date series by selecting an option in the **Date Unit** group.)

The end of a series is determined either by the number you supply as the **Stop Value**, or by the end of the selected range, whichever comes first.

 reminder

You can also use Excel's **AutoFill** feature to create some types of series on a worksheet. See *AutoFill* on page 4 for details.

Shading

Shading is a visual effect that you can use to highlight and emphasize important ranges of data on a worksheet.

To Apply Shading to a Worksheet Range

1. Select the range that you want to shade.

2. Choose **Format ➤ Cells**, and click the **Patterns** tab.

3. Click the arrow next to the **Pattern** box, and select a shading pattern from the drop-down list.

4. For shading in color, select a color from the palette in the **Cell Shading** box.

5. Click **OK** to apply the shading.

The worksheet in Figure 9 illustrates the use of shading to highlight selected ranges of values. See *Patterns* on page 88 for more information.

	A	B	C	D	E
1	XYZ Corp. Product Sales 1993				
2		Q1	Q2	Q3	Q4
3	Product 1	$7,373	$8,939	$6,850	$9,996
4	Product 2	$2,256	$5,801	$3,999	$2,733
5	Product 3	$9,478	$3,329	$4,480	$3,580
6	Product 4	$4,137	$8,756	$8,078	$8,157
7	Product 5	$7,761	$4,582	$6,347	$2,741
8	Product 6	$8,008	$3,954	$8,430	$3,471
9	Product 7	$7,253	$6,590	$8,833	$5,676
10	Product 8	$5,141	$4,005	$2,577	$4,748
11	Product 9	$4,395	$7,228	$2,743	$8,623
12	Product 10	$1,876	$2,052	$5,851	$1,321

FIGURE 9: *Using light shading to highlight worksheet ranges*

Shortcut Menus

The shortcut menus are designed to give you quick access to Excel's most commonly used menu commands. Shortcut menus are available for almost any item you work with in the Excel application window.

To Choose a Command from a Shortcut Menu

Point to a cell, a range, or another object in the Excel window, and click the right mouse button to view the corresponding shortcut menu. Then choose any available command in the menu.

 note

Most shortcut menus contain a selection of commands from Excel's **Edit** and **Format** menus. For example, the shortcut menu for a cell or range on a worksheet contains commands for cut-and-paste, copy-and-paste, deletions, insertions, and formatting operations. In addition, some shortcut menus contain special-purpose commands that apply to the specific item you are pointing to.

Sorting

⊚ ⊚ ⊚ ⊚ ⊚ ⊚ ⊚ ⊚ ⊚ ⊚ ⊚ ⊚ ⊚ ⊚ ⊚ ⊚ ⊚ ⊚ ⊚

The **Data ➢ Sort** command rearranges a range of worksheet data in alphabetical, numeric, or chronological order, or in a customized order that you choose. Although the sort command is best suited to rearranging the rows of a list or a database, you can also use the command to rearrange columns of data. Either way you can define as many as three keys for each sort operation.

To Sort a List or a Database

1. Activate the worksheet that contains the list and select any cell within the list.

2. Choose **Data ➤ Sort**. Excel selects all the records of the list and opens the **Sort** dialog box.

3. Click the down-arrow next to the **Sort by** box. The resulting drop-down list contains the names of all the fields in your table. Click the name of the field that will be the first key to the sort—that is, the column by which the list will be rearranged first.

4. Click **Ascending** or **Descending** for the first key. (See the notes below for an explanation of these two options.)

5. If you want to choose fields for the second and third sorting keys, repeat steps 3 and 4 to select fields in one or both of the **Then By** list boxes. Excel will use the second key to arrange records that contain identical entries in the first key; likewise, the third key is for sorting records that contain identical entries in the first and second keys.

6. Click **OK**. Excel carries out the sort that you have specified.

 shortcut

Select the list or database range and use the Tab key to activate a cell in the field that will be the key in the sort. Then click the **Sort Ascending** or **Sort Descending** button in the **Standard** toolbar.

 tip

For a key that contains text entries, the **Ascending** option sorts the data in alphabetical order and **Descending** sorts in reverse alphabetical order. For a key that contains date or time values, **Ascending** sorts in chronological order and **Descending** sorts in reverse chronological order.

reminder

You can undo a sort by choosing **Edit** ➤ **Undo Sort** (or by pressing **Ctrl+Z**) *immediately* after the sort operation.

recommended

When you design a large database that you intend to work with in a variety of sorted orders, consider including a *record number* field, where the values represent the original unsorted record order. You can then restore the original order by using this number field as a key. See *Database* on page 36 for more information.

Summation

Excel provides a special *summation* tool known as AutoSum. This tool is located on the Standard toolbar, and is labeled Σ. You can use AutoSum to calculate totals for rows and columns of numeric data. It automatically enters a SUM function in the cell at the bottom of a column of numbers, or to the right of a row of numbers. The SUM function in turn calculates the sum of all the values in the range.

To Use the AutoSum Tool

1. Select the cell just beneath a column of numbers, or just to the right of a row of numbers.

2. Click the **AutoSum** tool. Excel enters a SUM function into the formula bar. The function's argument is the numeric range just above or just to the left of the current cell.

3. If necessary, adjust the argument of the SUM function, either by pointing to a new range on the worksheet, or by editing the reference directly in the formula bar.

4. Press ↵ to enter the function into the selected cell.

recommended

If you don't need to change the SUM function before completing the entry, Excel provides a shortcut. Select a cell below or to the right of a range of numbers, and double-click the **Auto-Sum** tool. Excel determines an appropriate range argument for the SUM function, and enters the function into the current cell.

tip

To enter totals for several columns or rows of a table, select the row immediately beneath the table or the column just to the right of the table, and click the **AutoSum** tool once.

Figure 10 shows a monthly expense worksheet. To enter the monthly totals into row 8 and the expense category totals into column E of this worksheet, follow these steps:

1. Select B8:E8 and click the **AutoSum** tool.

2. Select E2:E8 and click the **AutoSum** tool again.

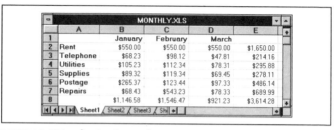

FIGURE 10: *Using the AutoSum tool*

Undo

⊙ ⊙ ⊙ ⊙ ⊙ ⊙ ⊙ ⊙ ⊙ ⊙ ⊙ ⊙ ⊙ ⊙ ⊙ ⊙ ⊙ ⊙ ⊙ ⊙

The **Edit ➤ Undo** command undoes the effect of your most
recent action. Undo is available for many—but not all—
operations in Excel.

To Undo the Most Recent Action

Choose **Edit ➤ Undo** *immediately* after the action that you want
to reverse.

shortcut

Ctrl+Z is the keyboard shortcut for **Edit ➤ Undo**.

tip

The **Edit ➤ Undo** command identifies the action that will be
reversed. For example, the command might be displayed as
Undo Font or **Undo Delete**.

ss

warning

If the command is dimmed or displayed as **Can't Undo**, the undo feature is not available for your last action.

recommended

After you choose **Edit ➤ Undo**, the first command in the **Edit** menu changes to **Redo**. Choose this command if you want to restore the effect of the action that you have just undone.

Window Operations

You can use familiar mouse techniques to adjust the size and position of workbook windows within Excel. In addition, several commands in the Window menu give you control over the appearance and organization of windows.

To Change the Size and Position of a Workbook Window

Use any of the following techniques:

- Drag any border or corner of the window to change the size and shape.

- Drag the title bar to move the window to a new position on the screen.

- Click the maximize button to expand a window's size to the entire available screen space.

⊛ Click the restore button to return to the previous size and position.

 reminder

A window's control menu shows a list of keyboard techniques for performing these same window operations. To view the control menu, click the window's control-menu box, or press **Alt+hyphen**.

To Activate the Window for an Open Workbook

Pull down the **Window** menu and choose the name of the workbook you want to activate.

To Open Multiple Windows for Viewing the Active Workbook

Select **Window** ➢ **New Window**.

 recommended

Multiple windows allow you to view different parts of a document at one time. When you open more than one window for a document, the title bar of each window displays the document's name, followed by a colon and the window number—for example, Book1:1 and Book1:2.

118

To Rearrange
Two or More Open Windows

1. Choose **Window ➤ Arrange**.

2. Click one of the options in the Arrange group: **Tiled**, **Horizontal**, **Vertical**, or **Cascade**.

3. If you want to arrange only the multiple windows of the active document, click the **Windows of Active Workbook** option. An X appears in the corresponding check box.

4. Click **OK**.

 tip

The **Tiled**, **Horizontal**, and **Vertical** arrangement options allow you to view multiple documents side-by-side or one above another.

To Close a Window

1. Activate the window that you want to close.

2. Choose **File ➤ Close**.

 shortcut

Another way to close a window is to double-click the window's control-menu box, located at the left side of the title bar.

warning

If you have made changes in the document since the last save, Excel asks you if you want to save the document. Click **Yes** to save, or **No** to abandon the changes. Alternatively, click **Cancel** to back out of the Close operation.

Workbooks

The workbook is the basic document type in Excel 5. A workbook may contain any combination of worksheets and chart sheets. If you make use of Excel's advanced programming capabilities, you'll also store macros, modules, and dialog sheets in workbooks. To activate any sheet in a workbook, you simply click the sheet's tab along the bottom border of the workbook window. Although each new workbook starts out with a standard number of worksheets, you are free to add or delete sheets according to the requirements of a particular document. You can use a workbook effectively to store and manage any number of interrelated worksheets, charts, and macros.

To Create a New Workbook

Choose **File ➤ New**.

shortcut

Click the **New Workbook** button on the **Standard** toolbar.

120

note

A new workbook has a default name like Book1, Book2, and so on. Initially each new workbook contains sixteen worksheets, named Sheet1 through Sheet16.

To Activate a Sheet in a Workbook

Click the sheet's tab at the bottom of the workbook window. If the tab is not visible for the sheet you want to activate, click any combination of the four tab scrolling buttons at the lower-left corner of the window to move other tabs into view.

Alternatively, press **Ctrl-PgDn** to activate the next sheet in the workbook, or **Ctrl-PgUp** to activate the previous sheet.

To Select Multiple Sheets in a Workbook

For contiguous sheets, click the tab of the first sheet in the selection, then hold down the **Shift** key and click the tab of the last sheet.

For noncontiguous sheets, hold down the **Ctrl** key while you click the tab of each sheet you want to include in the selection.

 see also

See *Links and 3-D Formulas* on page 67 for operations you can perform on multiple sheets in a workbook.

To Insert a Sheet into a Workbook

Pull down the **Insert** menu and choose **Worksheet**, **Chart**, or **Macro**, depending on the kind of sheet you want to add to your workbook. (Before you add a new chart sheet, you'll generally want to select the data upon which the chart will be based; see *Charting* on page 10 for details.)

 shortcut

Click any tab at the bottom of the workbook with the right mouse button. The workbook shortcut menu appears. Choose the **Insert** command, select a sheet type from the **Insert** dialog box, and click **OK**.

To Rename a Sheet in a Workbook

1. Activate the sheet that you want to rename.

2. Choose **Format** ➤ **Sheet**, and then click the **Rename** command in the **Sheet** submenu. The **Rename** dialog box appears on the screen.

3. Enter a new name for the sheet and click **OK**. The new name appears on the sheet's tab.

 shortcut

Double-click a sheet's tab to display the **Rename** dialog box.

To Move or Copy a Sheet

1. If you want to move or copy a sheet to a different work-book, open both the source workbook and the destination workbook. If you are moving a sheet to a new location within a workbook, only the target workbook need be open.

2. Activate the source workbook and click the tab for the sheet that you want to move or copy.

3. Choose **Edit** ➢ **Move** or **Copy Sheet**. The **Move** or **Copy** dialog box appears on the screen.

4. In the **To Book** list, select the name of the destination workbook. If you are copying or moving a sheet within one workbook, leave the name of the current workbook name as the **To Book** selection. To move or copy the active sheet to a new workbook, select the *(new book)* entry in the **To Book** list.

5. In the **Before Sheet** list, select the name of the sheet that will be located *after* the sheet that you are moving or copying.

6. To copy the sheet, check the **Create a Copy** option; to move the sheet, leave this option unchecked.

7. Click **OK**.

 shortcut

To move a sheet within its workbook, drag the sheet's tab to a new position in the row of tabs. When you release the mouse button, Excel moves the sheet. To copy a sheet within its workbook, hold down the **Ctrl** key while you drag the sheet's tab to a new position.

To move or copy a sheet to a different workbook, arrange the source and destination workbooks so that both can be seen at once, and drag the tab of the sheet from one workbook to the other. (To move the sheet, simply drag with the mouse to move the sheet. To copy the sheet, hold down the **Ctrl** key while you drag.)

To move or copy a sheet to a new workbook, drag the sheet's tab into the blank background area of the Excel window. (Hold down the **Ctrl** key if you want to copy the sheet.) Excel creates a new workbook, and moves or copies the target sheet into the new book.

To Hide a Sheet

Activate the sheet that you want to hide, and choose **Format** ➤ **Sheet**. Then click the **Hide** command from the resulting submenu.

To Delete a Sheet from a Workbook

Activate the sheet that you want to delete, and choose **Edit** ➤ **Delete Sheet**. Excel displays a warning box; click **OK** to confirm the deletion.

 shortcut

Click the sheet's tab with the right mouse button, and choose the **Delete** command from the shortcut menu. In the resulting warning box, click **OK** to confirm.

Zooming

The **View** ➤ **Zoom** command allows you to enlarge or reduce the viewing scale of a worksheet.

To Change the Scale of a Worksheet

1. Activate the worksheet that you want to view.

2. Choose **View** ➤ **Zoom**. The **Zoom** dialog box contains a group of **Magnification** option buttons.

3. Click one of the preset magnification or reduction options. Alternatively, click the **Custom** option, and enter a value from 10 to 400 in the **%** text box.

4. Click **OK** to apply the zoom scale.

The **View** ➤ **Zoom** command affects only the active sheet. Other sheets in the active workbook retain their current scale setting.

 tip

The **View** ➤ **Zoom** command is also available for chart sheets.

INDEX

Boldface page numbers indicate definitions and principal discussions of primary topics and subtopics. *Italic* page numbers indicate illustrations.

D

data. *See also* entries; values
   clearing procedures for, **18–20**
   copying from cells and
      ranges, **25, 26**
   entering into range, **46**
   linking with chart, 17–18
   moving with Cut and Paste
      commands, **74–75**
   replacing in worksheet,
      100–103
   searching for in worksheet,
      51–52
   selecting for chart, 17
database. *See also* database criteria;
      data form; filters; list
   creating, **36–37**
   criteria range creation for,
      37–38
   definition and use of, 36
   editing records in, **32**
   filtered, applying custom
      criteria to, **48–49**
   filtered, displaying all records
      in, **50**
   filtered, removing filter from,
      50
   filtering with AutoFilter,
      46–48
   for inventory control, 39
   record numbers for, 114
   removing filters from, **50**
   sorting, **112–114**
   viewing records in, 31
database criteria. *See also* database;
      filters
   comparison type, 35, **37–38**
   computed type, 37, **39**

   custom type, applying to
      filtered database, **48–49**
   establishing for records
      search, 34–35, 72
database criteria range. *See also*
      database; filters
   creating, **37–38**
   for filtering database, **50**
   use with Advanced Filter, 47
database functions. *See also* functions
   for statistical calculations,
      72–73
data form. *See also* database; list
   adding new records in, **33**
   closing, 31
   criteria use with, 35, 36
   for database operations, 72
   definition and use of, 30–31
   deleting records in, **34**
   editing records in, **32**
   maximum fields for, 32
   searching for records in,
      34–35, 72
   sorting records in, 33
   viewing records in, **31**
data table. *See also* data form;
      worksheets
   formats for, **6–7**
dates. *See also* numeric values;
      series
   consecutive, in series, 5
   determining difference
      between, **41**
   entering in worksheet cell,
      39–40
   formats for, **80**–81
   in headers or footers, **60–62**
   serial number representation
      of, 40–41

for formulas, **79–80**
function and uses for, **76**
for multiple-window documents, 118
Pasting into formulas, **79**
renaming workbook sheet, **122**
for workbook components, 61–62
notes. *See also* labels; text
creating and viewing, **19**
deleting from worksheet, **18–20**
in printed worksheets, 84
searching for in worksheet, **51–52**
numbers. *See also* numeric values
formats for, **80–81**, 81
numeric values. *See also* entries; serial number; text
alignment of in cells or ranges, **1–2**
comparison criteria as, 38
deleting from worksheet, **18**
entering into worksheet, **56**
formatting for, 6–7, **55**
formatting in worksheet, **80–81**
as names, 78
serial numbers as, 81
series for, 5
summation procedures for, **114–116**

O

opening. *See also* closing; exiting
files, **82**
workbooks, **83**

operands. *See also* arithmetic operations; formulas
for arithmetic formula, **4**
selecting for formulas, 57
Outline, in border selection, 7

P

page, previewing, **89–90**, 90
page breaks, manual, **94–95**
page numbers
in headers or footers, **60–62**
for printed worksheets, 84–85
Page Setup
changing page layout, 94
printing worksheet, **83–85**, 89
panes
dividing worksheets into, **85–87**, 86
freezing in split worksheets, 87
removing from worksheet, **87–88**
passwords, creating for restricted access, 106
Paste command. *See also* copying; moving
copying data, **25**
keyboard shortcuts for, 25–26, 75
pasting names into formulas, **79**
undoing, 30
paths. *See also* Directories; punctuation
finding for files, 82
patterns. *See also* colors; fills; shading
applying shading to cells, **88**

140

Standard toolbar

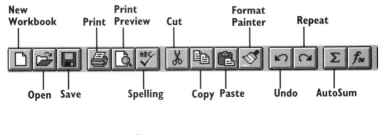

New Workbook | Print | Print Preview | Cut | Format Painter | Repeat
Open | Save | Spelling | Copy | Paste | Undo | AutoSum

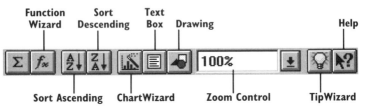

Function Wizard | Sort Descending | Text Box | Drawing | Help
Sort Ascending | ChartWizard | Zoom Control | TipWizard

Formatting toolbar

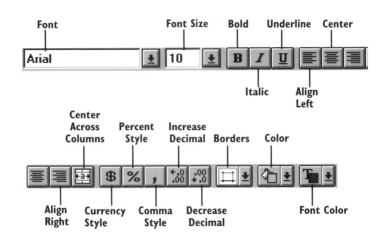

Font | Font Size | Bold | Underline | Center
Italic | Align Left

Center Across Columns | Percent Style | Increase Decimal | Borders | Color
Align Right | Currency Style | Comma Style | Decrease Decimal | Font Color